SOME ASPECTS OF THE
RELIGIOUS MUSIC
OF THE UNITED STATES NEGRO

INTERNATIONAL FOLKLORE

Advisory Editor
Richard M. Dorson

Editorial Board
Issachar Ben Ami
Vilmos Voigt

*See last pages of this volume
for a complete list of titles*

SOME ASPECTS
OF THE RELIGIOUS MUSIC
OF THE UNITED STATES NEGRO
An Ethnomusicological Study
with Special Emphasis
on the Gospel Tradition

George Robinson Ricks

ARNO PRESS

A New York Times Company

New York / 1977

Editorial Supervision: LUCILLE MAIORCA

———◆———

First Publication 1977 by Arno Press Inc.

Copyright © 1960 by George Robinson Ricks

Reprinted by permission of George Robinson Ricks

Reprinted from a copy in
  The Northwestern University Library

INTERNATIONAL FOLKLORE
ISBN for complete set: 0-405-10077-9
See last pages of this volume for titles.

Manufactured in the United States of America

Publisher's Note: This volume has been
reprinted from the best available copy.

———◆———

Library of Congress Cataloging in Publication Data

Ricks, George Robinson.
  Some aspects of the religious music of the United
States Negro.

  Originally presented as the author's thesis, Northwestern University, 1960.
  Bibliography: p.
  1. Negro music--History and criticism. 2. Gospel
music--History and criticism. I. Title.
ML3556.R43 1977   781.7'73   77-70621
ISBN 0-405-10123-6

NORTHWESTERN UNIVERSITY

SOME ASPECTS OF THE RELIGIOUS MUSIC
OF THE UNITED STATES NEGRO:
An Ethnomusicological Study with
Special Emphasis on the Gospel Tradition

A DISSERTATION

SUBMITTED TO THE GRADUATE SCHOOL

IN PARTIAL FULFILLMENT OF THE REQUIREMENTS

for the degree

DOCTOR OF PHILOSOPHY

Field of Anthropology

By

GEORGE ROBINSON RICKS

Evanston, Illinois

June, 1960

TABLE OF CONTENTS

LIST OF TABLES

PREFACE

The following study is concerned with the religious
music tradition of the United States Negro. Initially
the research dealt strictly with the contemporary gospel
style of Negro religious music and was orientated toward
an objective description of that style. However, under
the guidance of Professor Alan P. Merriam, the need for
an approach broader than pure analytic description on
a single time-plane was appreciated, and the decision
to add historic depth, including socio-cultural background and the relation of the contemporary style to
antecedent musical practices, has made this study an
attempt, at least, to present the well-rounded approach
conceived for Afroamerican studies by Professor Melville
J. Herskovits.

To facilitate this approach, both field and library
research were required. I was fortunate in having spent
considerable time in the early 1940's traveling through
the deep South (South Carolina, Georgia, Mississippi,
Alabama, Florida, Louisana, and Texas), and as a com-
municant of Negro Baptist faith enjoyed the role of a
participant observer. For purposes of comparison and af-
firmation of impressions gained from earlier experiences,
several months were spent in various southern cities
(Baltimore, Maryland; Washington, D.C.; Richmond and

Lynchburg, Virginia; Florence and Huntsville, Alabama;
Corinth, Mississippi; and Chattanooga, Memphis, and
Nashville, Tennessee) during the summer of 1954.

From 1955 to 1957 intensive field research and tape
recording was done in the Negro Community of Chicago,
Illinois. In addition to residing in this area, experiences as a social caseworker and school teacher in the
neighborhoods of immigrant Negro families were helpful
in gaining the rapport and orientation necessary for
this phase of the project. The choirs of some twenty-
one churches were recorded during services, rehearsals
and special programs, and some forty small groups,
including visiting musicians from Detroit, New York City,
Birmingham, Atlanta, Vicksburg, Oakland, Gary, Brooklyn,
and Memphis, were recorded on tape.

Musicians, composers, publishers and laymen
conversant with the field of Negro religious music were
used as informants, and these included such well qualified persons as Mahalia Jackson, singer Sallie Martin,
pianist-organist Charles Walker, composer-publisher-
musician Thomas A. Dorsey, composer-publisher Kenneth
Morris and the famous Beal Street historian Lieutenant
George W. Lee (in Memphis, Tennessee).

Library research was done at Howard University
(Washington, D.C.), The Library of Congress (Washington,
D.C.), Fisk University (Nashville, Tennessee), North-

western University (Evanston, Illinois), Hall Branch of the Chicago Public Library (Negro collection) and Newberry Library (Chicago, Illinois).

Grateful acknowledgment is given to the Department of Anthropology at Northwestern University, where my study of cultural anthropology was pursued, for making available the facilities of the Laboratory of Comparative Musicology. It would be difficult to make individual acknowledgments to all persons who have made contributions to this study. However, special appreciation must be given to Professor Melville J. Herskovits, who suggested the area of investigation, whose theoretical and methodological approach to studies in the Afroamerican field are basic to this project, and whose patience and understanding is remarkable. To Professor Alan P. Merriam, who not only helped to focus the anthropological frame of reference, but also guided the manuscript through its several stages and made many valuable criticisms and suggestions relative to the musicological transcriptions and analyses, my debt is immeasurable. My gratitude is also expressed to Professor Raymond W. Mack, whose extremely pertinent suggestions relative to the sociological aspects of this study have been most helpful; Dr. Frank B. Cookson whose critical reading of the manuscript and musical transcriptions have proved to be of vital importance to the final form of this work; and Doctor Richard A. Waterman who interested me in cultural anthropology during my studies for the Master's degree in Music at Northwestern University.

Further acknowledgment and appreciation is expressed to Mrs. Dorothy Porter, curator of the Moorland Collection at Founders Library, Howard University, for making available many useful references; Mr. Charles Walker, Mr. Thomas A. Dorsey, Miss Mahalia Jackson, Mr. Kenneth Morris and Miss Sallie Martin for imparting valuable knowledge and insight into the development of the contemporary gospel style of Negro religious music; Mr. Charles D. Warren who aided in proofreading the final manuscript; and to my wife Edith who has endured with patience the inevitable sacrifices.

Finally, in deep appreciation of their encouragement and assistance in furthering my academic career, I dedicate this work to my parents.

I. INTRODUCTION

Ethnomusicology, as one of the specialized branches
of the science of anthropology, has reflected in its
history various points of view as to the nature of culture. For example, when the nineteenth century concept
of cultural evolution and the search for cultural origins
dominated anthropological thought, the first serious
studies of the music of nonliterate peoples were similarly orientated. The works of Baker (1882) and
Wallaschek (1893) are typical of those which reflected
the evolutionists' point of view. Both scholars speculated
about the origin of music. Baker, in developing a classi-
ficatory scheme for song types on the basis of usage,
conceived of two musical styles (rhythmical dance and
recitative) as representing developmental stages of music.
Wallaschek followed this hypothetical assumption and
offered the postulate that "the origin of music is to be
sought in a general desire for rhythmical exercise..."
(Wallaschek 1893:294). Later, the influence of the
Kulturhistorische Schule (German-Austrian culture-historical
school) is seen in the writing of Von Hornbostel (1911:
601-615) which suggests, on solid musicological basis, an
historical relationship between Melanesian and Peruvian
cultures.

The contemporary anthropological point of view,

which focuses upon the dynamics of culture and upon observed culture change, has also exerted its influence upon ethnomusicology, and this influence is evidenced by the studies of McAllester (1949), Merriam (1951), and Waterman (1943).

The present work follows the latter students in their approach to comparative musicological investigation and, as in the case of Waterman and Merriam, uses the Afroamerican field as an area of concentration. In Afroamerican studies the investigator is afforded an unusual degree of control over the variables present in any study of culture change. Studies of New World Negroes in their varied socio-cultural setting may be projected against the knowledge of indigenous African cultures, thus creating a laboratory situation in which a controlled study of culture change is possible. The use of historical documents concerned with the slave trade, and accounts of life during that period, add to these studies a time dimension which helps to throw light on the processes by which change occurred. Thus, by the use of ethnohistory the study may estimate the effect of the variables of socio-cultural and ecological setting upon an established base-line of African culture and gain insights into the processes of culture change.

As a research tool ethnomusicology has great utility for the science of culture, especially in respect to study of the processes of acculturation, in that music can be

studied objectively and measured precisely. This aspect
of culture is highly susceptible to objective analysis
in many of its aspects--tempo, meter, interval usage,
rhythmic patterns, and other components--and when such
elements of raw musical data are analyzed under laboratory
conditions, they yield measurements which can be quanti-
tatively recorded. Further, since patterns of musical
expression are the products of unconscious conditioning
and have no great dependency upon ecological or social
setting for their survival, they tend to possess a considerable degree of stability. This persistence of
musical traits is further implemented in that such traits are
least likely to be the object of forced change even in cases
of dominant-subordinate cultural relations.

A case is point is that of the United States Negro
under slavery. Here, music was not the object of much
forceful supression; only the use of drums, after an extended period, was viewed with suspicion and subdued. While
the ecological and social setting called for drastic revision,
and in some cases abandonment, of other traditions, music
was either tolerated by representatives of the dominant
culture or, as in most cases, encouraged. In general, music
was one of the aspects of culture in which Negro slaves were
allowed great freedom of choice in accepting or rejecting
new elements. The music of slaves was used as entertainment
and as a means of increasing work; some of its characteristics

were even incorporated into the musical idiom of the dominant
group. Thus, the retention of the African musical traits
among the slaves was enhanced, in part, because of the
tolerant attitude of exponents of the dominant culture toward
their music.

The present study will be confined to the religious
musical tradition of the United States Negro. The development of this tradition of sacred music is not difficult to
comprehend when viewed in terms of (1) the phenomena of acceptance and rejection and (2) the process of musical syncretism. Like other aspects of Negro music, sacred music is the
product of a long-term, first-hand contact situation in the
New World between the musical traditions of Europe and Africa.
Although African slaves were the carriers of a musical tradition characterized by marked specific differences from
European music, the similarities were sufficient to allow
the slaves to incorporate elements of European music into
their indigenous style of music (Waterman 1952:209-10).
With the presence of a common rudimentary musical base for
African tribal and European folk music (Ibid.:209) syncretism was more possible here than in the case of other less
compatible musical styles[1] (Merriam 1955a).

[1]From his studies of the acculturative musical situation in terms of Western music and Flathead Indian music,
and Western music and that of Urban Africa south of the
Sahara Merriam concludes: "Western and Flathead musical
systems having little in common have...exchanged virtually
no ideas...for the two systems are simply not compat-

Change from a pure African musical style was of course
not immediate, but was rather a gradual development molded
by time and historic events. The forceful suppression of the
musical tradition of slaves in the United States was di-
rected mainly toward the use of drums and even this was
not a complete suppression. The continued use of drums after
the ban on their use, which dates from colonial times
(Franklin 1947:75), has been documented for various places.
Cable, for example, describes the scene at Congo Square in
New Orleans where slaves were allowed by special permission
to hold dances and celebrations in which drums were used:

> The booming of African drums and blast of huge
> wooden horns called to the gathering....The drums
> were very long, hollowed, often from a single
> piece of wood, open at one end and having a sheep
> or goat skin stretched across the other. One was
> large the other much smaller. The tight skin
> heads were not held up to be struck; the drums
> were laid along the turf and the drummers be-
> strode them and beat them on the head madly with
> fingers, fists and feet--with slow vehemence on
> the great drums and fiercely and rapidly on the
> small one. Sometimes an extra performer sat on
> the ground behind the larger drum, at its open
> end and beat upon the wooden sides of it with
> two stick. The smaller drum was often made
> from a joint or two of very large bamboo, in the
> West Indies where such could be got, and this is
> said to be the origin of its name; for it was
> called the Bamboula (Cable 1885:517).

Again, a former slave from the coastal area of Georgia
tells of the use of drums purely for religious purposes:

> ible. On the other hand, African and Western music, having
> a great deal in common, are mutually influential upon one
> another" (Merriam 1955a:34).

"Yuh needs a drum fuh shoutin'...We beat a drum at duh
church an' we beat a drum on duh way tuh duh grabe yard
tuh bury um. We walks in a long line moanin' an' we beats
duh drum all duh way" (Georgia Writers Project 1940:149).

First-hand acquaintance with the Euroamerican hymn
tradition, which began with the proselyting of slaves
in the Colonial period, did not result in the complete
acceptance of the concepts of hymnology offered by various
sects. There was not an immediate and complete abandonment
of African musical traits in favor of those of Western
culture. African tunes were remembered and used (Murphy
1899:660-661); some have been cited as late as 1942 for the
somewhat isolated Negro communities of the Georgia Sea Islands (Parrish 1942:45). The early forms of United States
Negro sacred song, which were unstable in terms of melody,
text, and harmony, were more than a century in developing
into the fully harmonized and standardized forms noted after
the Civil War[1] (Herskovits 1958:268), and took an additional

[1]M. J. Herskovits, (1958:268), takes significant notice
of the presence of European and African musical elements in
these stablized song forms when he cites the results of
Kolinski's analysis and comparison of West African songs
and United States Negro spirituals: "From the songs appearing in several such volumes of spirituals, thirty-six were
found to have the same scales (tonal structures) as specific
songs in the West African collection, while identical
correspondences in melodic line were even found in a few
instances. Thirty-four spirituals had the same rhythmic
structure as some of the West African melodies, while the
formal structure of fifty spirituals...their phrasing and
time...were found to have African counterparts."

three-quarters of a century in developing into the urban
style found among contemporary Negroes. It was a gradual
re-working of borrowed elements into the framework of
African musical style, forming a new tradition which embodies
the characteristics of both African and European musical
systems, that has given form to successive developments in
the United States Negro religious music.

Among some Negroes there was early acceptance of
Euroamerican musical values in sacred music. In pre- and
post-Emancipation times the "best" Negro churches used the
hymns of Watts and Wesley as well as those of the Moody and
Sankey tradition. Speaking of differences to be found in
Negro churches, Macrae reveals the situation in what he
calls the "best" Negro churches:

> Before the war this church was presided over by a
> white minister; but since the Negroes have got the
> power to elect for themselves, they have elected a
> pastor of their own colour. The service was very
> much like that of a white congregation, saving in
> one or two particulars. The hymns were sung with
> unusual fervour...The hymns were mostly Isaac
> Watts; and the sermon would have passed muster in
> many white churches (Macrae 1870:70).

The tradition in music found in these churches was
accelerated by the post-Civil War establishment of Negro
schools by various religious organizations and the Freedmen's Bureau. However, these students were developed into
trained choirs which sang highly stylized and arranged
versions of songs that robbed the music of its folk song
quality and made it more compatible with Euroamerican music

valued. The singing of the Fisk Jubilee Singers, for example,
was often criticized by those who had heard singing by untrained, unsophisticated Negro singers as being "too refined
and having too nice a balancing of the parts, and too much
delicate shading to be a genuine representation of slave
music" (Seward 1872:3). Theodore F. Seward, who came to
assist George L. White in the direction of the Jubilee
Singers in 1875, pointed out that these singers had "received
considerable musical instruction and have become familiar
with much of our best sacred and classical music and this
has modified their manner of execution" (Ibid.:79). The
rendition of choirs, like those of Fisk, Hampton, and
Tuskegee, were the beginnings of the art form of Negro religious song which made famous such Negro composers as Harry
T. Burleigh and R. Nathaniel Dett.

A large majority of Negroes, on the other hand, was
apparently less inclined to accept intrusion upon their
past musical practices, and this group included those individuals who, because of low social status, limited education
or relative isolation, experienced a condition which
strengthened their resistance toward change and exhibited
a greater retention of aboriginal musical customs. These
people, with conservative cultural outlook, continued the
folk development of the basic musical tradition which grew
out of a syncretism of African and Euroamerican musical
elements.

Thus, there were two traditions in the use of sacred music among Negroes. On one hand we have a tradition which embraces the Euroamerican hymn style and uses an academic approach in the development of an art form of Negro sacred song. On the other hand we have a tradition in which the folk development of Negro sacred song is dominant. These two traditions existed among early Negroes, and, influenced by varying degrees of social and geographical isolation, have been carried over into the present in family and group tradition.

Failure to recognize the existence of the two traditions, and further, failure to recognize that the forms of the folk tradition were subject to change, caused many observers to mourn prematurely the abandonment of the folk tradition by Negroes. Brown (1868:617) noted shortly after the Civil War that "the round of sacred song...so familiar... throughout the southern states is now fading from use and remembrance. It is giving place to a totally different system of words and melody" (Brown 1868:67). Other observers (Macrae 1870:78; Haskel 1899:377) also referred to the passing of this tradition and held that its disappearance was due to increasing educational opportunities for Negroes.

Evidence indicates, however, that the folk tradition, in spite of an increase in educational opportunity for Negroes, had not been fading in favor of a complete acceptance by Negroes of Moody and Sankey hymns. In the first

place, while the educational status of the Negro improved
after 1865, the degree of education which, in combination
with other factors might have been sufficient to obliterate
a deeply rooted musical tradition, was available only to a
small proportion of the total Negro population. As phrased
by one writer, more than a quarter of a century after
Emancipation:

> There are today 2,250,000 Negroes who have learned
> to read. This is indeed a remarkable fact. The
> 11th census gives us a total of 6,996,166 Negroes
> in the United States and by a simple process in
> arithmetic we discover that there are some 4,746,166
> uneducated Negroes in the Southern states (Ryder
> 1892:9).

Further, accounts of other observers in the late nineteenth
century and later, support the continued existence of the
folk tradition, especially in the South and even in large
cities "where schools have been sustained for years" (Anon
1890:82). Post-Civil War descriptions of sacred song and
dance point out the continued tradition of a distinctive
Negro folk style which characterized the music found in
rural churches, camp meetings, and the shouting churches in
cities (Kilham 1870:309; Murphy 1899:661; Showers 1898:481;
Barton 1899:707).

Changes in musical style appear to be coincident with
certain changes in the Negro's social and economic conditions
and place of residence. One change, which occurred shortly
after Emancipation, has been pointed out. A second, which
grew out of the gradual effects of Emancipation and has

influenced the contemporary style of sacred music, was the urbanization of the Negro.

For almost three centuries United States Negroes had been concentrated in a southern-rural setting. As Myrdal (1944:182) points out:

> Ever since they were brought to this country as slaves, Negroes have been concentrated in the South. There had been little use for slaves in the North and the Northern state governments early abolished what slavery there was. The South, on the other hand, after an initial period of experimentation, came to regard slavery as an essential part of its economy, and brought Negroes in as long as it was legally possible to do so, and after that bred and smuggled them to increase the number of slaves.

In 1860 almost ninety-five per cent of the Negro population of the United States was still in the South and more than eighty per cent lived in rural-plantation areas (U.S. Bureau of the Census 1860:i,xiii). Even in the first decade of the twentieth century the greatest portion of the Negroes was found in a southern-rural environment, but following the "Great Migration" significant changes in the geographical distribution of Negroes took place. Kennedy's study (1930:23-32) of Negro population movements of this period (1910-1920) reveals significant changes in Negro migration patterns. Whereas movements had been confined mostly within the South, there was now a trend toward northward migration and a further tendency to concentrate in the largest cities both North and South.

The census statistics of 1930 (U.S. Bureau of Census

1930:11,27) reveal that by this time over forty per cent
of all Negroes were to be found in urban areas while
about thirty-six per cent were living in rural non-farm
areas. A decade later, over one-fifth of the total Negro
population was found in the urban North, approximately
fifty per cent of which was located in six large cities:
New York, Philadelphia, Chicago, Detroit, Cleveland, and
Pittsburgh. Including the urban population in the South,
about fifty per cent of the Negroes in the United States
were urban dwellers (U.S. Bureau of the Census 1940:11,13-19).
Since World War II, sizable migrations from the South to the
urban North and West have further increased the percentage
of urban Negroes, and in 1950, of the more than ten million
Negroes fourteen years and older, more than seven million
were classed as urban dwellers (U.S. Bureau of the Census
1950:27).

The response of the once predominantly rural Negro
to urbanization, with its concomitants of extended education,
altered social setting, and improved economic status, has
meant new adaptive measures in terms of culture; and, as
with other aspects of culture, music has manifested a
response to change from rural farm or plantation life to
urban living. In the early 1900's an urban tradition in
Negro religious music deeply rooted in the Negro folk tradition, was found to be developing among the less educated,
lower classes in the shouting churches. A written form

has developed and spread to many rural areas as well as to urban orthodox Negro churches, challenging and often replacing the "old spiritual jubilee" forms and the Moody-Sankey type hymns. This Negro religious music, termed "Gospel," is of chief concern here. It is a contemporary form which reflects the influences of previous musical styles and appears to be an amalgam of much that has developed in Negro music. The accumulated material of antecedent Negro musical developments upon which it has drawn, is the result of the synthesis of African and European styles of music.

Statement of the Problem

Today, as in the past, Negroes in the United States are identified with various religious denominations which coincide with differences in social status and which vary in religious behavior and practice. Among these social classes and denominations distinct musical styles are found, and there thus appears to be a correlation between social class, church affiliation, and adherence to a particular tradition in sacred music.

The style of music most characteristic of the churches of the lower classes exhibits the greatest difference from the norms of the Euroamerican hymnology, since most of the songs used for worship are from the repertory of the Negro folk tradition, and since those Euroamerican hymns which are used are generally adapted to this folk style. Thus, we may expect to find a close correspondence between the

religious music of present-day churches and the tradition
of those similar religious bodies of the past, among which
the "spiritual-jubilee" tradition developed. External
evidence indicates that there is such a correlation, since
the new songs are often referred to as "New Day Spirituals,"
and since they differ from the art forms of Negro religious
music in that they are a folk development rather than arranged music governed by the strict discipline of European
music theory and harmony.

The analysis of contemporary urban Negro sacred music
poses two major problems: (1) a definition of the contemporary style, and (2) the establishment of its background
in terms of its relationship to antecedent forms. Hence,
the aims of this study are (1) to obtain a quantitative
description of the existing forms of the tradition by means
of musicological analysis, and (2) to determine their relationships by musicological comparison. As a result of
this analysis and comparison two other fundamental questions
may be answered: (1) Has the contemporary tradition shifted
away from the basic musical values characteristically expressed in antecedent forms? and (2) Has there been a retention of old elements and development of new elements?

The degree of communication among adherents of the
contemporary style has been hampered but little, if at all,
by geographical distance. Close lines of communication have
been effected by traveling groups, commercial recordings,

radio programs, a national organization of gospel choruses, and a school of gospel music and printed music; thus a high degree of uniformity in style has been achieved. Chicago is the focus of activity in gospel music among Negroes. The style started here, and it is the publishing center of Negro gospel songs as well as the headquarters of the national organization and school of music. In addition, the constant influx of immigrants from many s tates and the regular visits of professional groups from major cities provide representative examples of style. These factors have influenced the samples of musical data and provided for a high degree of control over the variables. In view of the above factors and since the musical data used is selected from performances sanctioned by musicians and adherents of the musical tradition as representative of the styles extant, the conclusions of this study, in terms of musicological analysis, may be held valid for the United States Negro religious music tradition in general.

II. THE EARLY PERIOD

In order to obtain an understanding of the contemporary religious music of the urban United States Negro it is necessary to examine its stylistic characteristics and the conditions under which they appeared in the different periods of the Negro's musical history in the United States. The periods may be delineated as follows: (1) Early (pre-Civil War), (2) Middle (post-Civil War), and (3) Late (Early 1900's to date). The chronological limits of each style are not assumed to be rigid, for while they precede one another in time they are continuous and overlapping, and thus the music of the early period has served as an inspiration and guide for musical creations of the two subsequent periods, and that of the late period has drawn upon material of the two preceding periods for substance.

Regional Setting

From the beginning of Negro slavery in the United States, the greatest concentration of Negroes has been in the rural South, since slaves formed the largest portion of the Negro population and were an essential part of southern plantation economy. The first Federal Census (1790) estimates the total Negro population at 757,000, of which about 59,000 were free Negroes (U.S. Bureau of the Census 1870:1,6). By 1860 this population had increased to an estimated 4,442,000,

16.

of which only some 500,000 were free (Ibid.), and in 1860
practically the total Negro population (94.9%) in the United
States was to be found in the South (U.S. Bureau of the
Census 1860:1,xiii). Even after Emancipation the largest
part of the Negro population, some four-fifths, was living
in the rural South (Myrdal 1944:185).

Education

For the most part, the education of the Negroes was
either neglected or prohibited and this attitude toward
their education persisted until the first half of the
nineteenth century. The efforts of such groups as the
Society for the Propagation of the Gospel in Foreign Parts,
and the Society of Friends (Quakers), to give instruction
to Negroes met with little success, since the southern planter
either feared or felt little need for the education of his
slaves. Increasing slave insurrections and escapes rein-
forced the opposition to education or religious instruction,
and as a result, less than 1.7 per cent of the total Negro
population was receiving formal education before the Civil
War (U.S. Bureau of the Census 1870:1,396-97).

Negroes in this period experienced varying degrees
of access to Euroamerican culture and thus exhibited varying
degrees of adaptation, acceptance, and integration of Euroamerican behavior patterns and values (Herskovits 1958:
123-24). The experience of United States Negroes differed
as to the extent and kind of contact with representatives

of the dominant culture. In those regions of the United
States where there was a high numerical ratio of Negroes to
whites, such as in the Sea Islands (Johnson 1930:127) and
the "low country" of Georgia and South Carolina (Anon 1872a:
22), or where plantations were somewhat isolated in the back
country (Olmstead 1904:I,118), Negroes were noticeably less
inclined to the ways of Euroamerican culture. Negro inhabitants in the "low country," for example, were held in many
ways to be distinctly less Western in their cultural behavior than those in other parts of the South, and were viewed
by one observer to be "the purest specimens of the native
unadulterated African on Southern soil" (Anon 1872:22).
Similarly, differences between the rural and the urban Negro
were recognized, the latter being viewed as generally more
sophisticated and educated than his country counterpart.

Social Classes

Class distinctions among slaves were recognized in
several ways. One criteria for measuring a slave's social
status was the position of his owner in the general plantation social hierarchy, and thus slaves belonging to the
better class of planters assumed a higher status than those
of less respected planters. Anderson, a former slave, describes this association of a slave's status to that of his
owner in the following words:

> The slaves belonging to the lower class of white
> folks, were not considered on the same level as
> those belonging to the quality folks and the slaves

of these families were always proud of and bragged
of their connection with the better families
(Anderson 1927:19).

There was also assumed class distinction among slaves
based upon house and field positions. Observers have noted
that house servants were often regarded as "privileged
class" (Steward 1857:32) and by assumed manners and dress,
in addition to the distinction of not being under the lash
of the slave driver, created a kind of social distance between themselves and the field hands.

> The house-servants held themselves at an immeasurable
> distance above the field-hand and would tell with
> an air of superiority infinitely amusing, that 'dey
> nebber done no common work, dey was allus roun' de
> house jest under missis' orders'; their social standing
> being settled, in their own estimation, as nearly as
> I could make out, by the fact of their having been,
> or having not been under an overseer (Kilham 1870:
> 205).

The difference in this case appears to be one of a
higher status ascribed to the house servant because of a
more "favored" position in the plantation system, rather
than because of exclusive knowledge of the patterns and
values of the dominant culture. As a matter of course,
house servants had the advantage of closer contact with the
home life of their owners and learned from their conversa-
tions and from observation (Clarke 1846:15-16). As revealed from the experience of a former slave:

> Being employed in the kitchen helping to cook, or
> waiting table, and listening to the conversation
> going on, I learned many things of which the field
> hands were entirely ignorant (Frederick 1869:15).

Exclusion from the household, however, was not an impassable
barrier to the field hand, for there was much transfer of
knowledge between the household and field slave. During the
time away from labor, especially on holidays when slaves were
allowed to gather for celebrations, information was passed
on from one group of slaves to another. As Stewart reveals:

> The field hands and such of them as have generally
> been excluded from the dwelling of their owners
> looked to the house servant as a pattern of polite-
> ness and gentility and indeed as the only method
> of obtaining any knowledge of the manners of what
> is called genteel society (Steward 1857:31-32).

Though viewed as paragons of Western cultural behavior, house
servants were seen to "break down" to the music played for
dancing and revert to indigenous patterns of behavior, performing "with all the wild abandon of the African character"
(Stewart 1857:33).

Patterns of Religious Expression

There were three types of churches in the religious
experiences of these United States Negroes: (1) the mixed
church attended by both Negroes and whites, (2) the separate
church under white leadership, and (3) the all-Negro church.
The mixed church seems to have developed from the activities
of missionary societies such as the Society for Promoting
Religious Knowledge Among the Poor and The Society for
Propagating the Gospel in Foreign Parts, whose custom it was
to preach to mixed, though separated, audiences of poor
farmers and slaves. Foote reveals an early situation in a

letter under the date of March 1775:

> The inhabitants of Virginia are computed to be
> about 300,000 men, the one-half of which are
> supposed to be negroes. The number of those who
> attend my ministry at particular times is...gene-
> rally about 300...and never have I been so struck
> with the appearance of an assembly, as when I have
> glanced my eye to that part of the meeting house
> where they usually sit adorned...with so many
> black countenances (Foote 1850:285).

This practice of mixed congregations continued into the
middle decades of the nineteenth century, and Olmstead,
describing his trip through the South in the early 1850's
tells of a church service attended by Negroes and whites:

> The religious service...was held in a less than
> usually rude meetinghouse...about one-third of the
> house...was covered by a gallery or cock-loft,
> under and in which distinctly separated from the
> whites was a dense body of negroes; the men on
> one side the women on another. The whites were
> seated promiscuously in the body of the house
> (Olmstead 1904:II,85).

The separate church under white leadership was also
a common practice and was frequently organized around
the itinerant minister who visited plantations and conducted services for the slaves. On most plantations, slaves
were provided with a small chapel, often a rude brush arbor
or log structure (Fuller 1938:1; Olmstead 1904:II,80) in
which these services were held. There were also churches
for Negroes, under white leadership, in towns.(Olmstead
Ibid.).

The all-Negro church apparently developed between
the latter decades of the eighteenth century and the early

part of the nineteenth century. The first known church of
this kind was one of Baptist denomination organized near
Savannah, Georgia, about 1778, and other all-Negro churches
were subsequently organized in Georgia and other parts of the
South (Simms 1888:1). In the first two decades of the nineteenth century all-Negro churches of two other denominations
were organized and, along with the Negro Baptists, are still
in force today: the African Methodist Episcopal Church (Philadelphia, 1816) and the African Methodist Episcopal Zion Church
(New York City, 1820) (Woodson 1921:65,72). In the South,
before the Civil War, the meetings of all-Negro churches were
observed closely by persons assigned to prevent plans for
escape or revolt; thus Olmstead observed that "they are not
allowed to have meetings without some white man present. They
must not preach unless a white man hears what they say,
however, they do" (Olmstead 1904:II,80). McIllhenny relates
an account of such secret meetings as told by an ex-slave:

> Fo' de war we'd have a meeting' at night, wuz
> mos' always 'way in de woods or de bushes some
> whar so de white folks couldn't hear an' when
> dey'd sing a spiritual an de spirit 'gin to
> shout some de elders would go 'mongst de folks
> an' put dey hand over dey mouth an' sometimes
> put a cloth in dey mouth an' say "Spirit don'
> talk so loud or de patterol break us up"
> (McIllhenny 1910:30).

Among members of the slave population who were less inclined toward the patterns of Western culture, religious
meetings were pheonomena of a different order from those
found in the Negro churches that followed the observance

of orthodox Protestantism in the United States. The scenes
observed are described as primarily emotional in character,
taking the form of leaping, screaming, hand-clapping, and
dancing (Olmstead, 1904:II,80). Macrae observed that among
this group "all their religious exercises partake of this
exciting character and in some of their churches a service
seems to be regarded as a kind of failure unless the audience
gets itself worked up to a frenzy...These excitements, more
particularly when they occur during the service of praise
are called 'shoutings'" (Macrae 1870:70). This "shouting"
tradition developed into an institution among the large
masses of culturally conservative Negroes in contrast to
the religious worship of the group that adhered more closely
to the liturgy and doctrines of the Protestant church.
Macrae took notice of this contrast:

> In the best churches these scenes do not occur
> (shouting)...the services are very much like
> that of a white congregation...The hymns sung
> were mostly Isaac Watts; and the sermon would
> have passed muster in many white churches...But
> at the camp meetings, and in the little wooden
> churches and booths in which the negroes congre-
> gate in country districts, the services are
> very peculiar and tend much more to excitement
> than edification. The hymns sung are generally
> original, and are of so simple a structure that
> they can be spun out with ease to any length,
> according to the spirit of the worshippers...
> (Macrae, Ibid.).

Patterns of Religious Musical Expression

The characteristics of the music found in the "shouting"
tradition in Negro religion are of primary concern here.

The relationship of their musical idiom, as a part of United
States Negro musical expression in general, to that of
Africa has already been pointed out (Merriam 1952, Waterman
1952). However, it seems profitable to discuss briefly the
theoretical reasoning through which the anthropologist views
the persistence of characteristic African musical traits in
this New World Negro idiom.

To the anthropologist, cultural behavior, in musical
as well as other terms, is learned (Herskovits 1948:625-28),
and once a behavior pattern is learned it is difficult to
eliminate. In respect to the musical aspect of culture, the
conditioning of individuals by the learning process is so
subtle, yet so thorough, as to effect a kind of unconscious
behavior (Ibid. 435). In the case of the African slave, music
was of great importance in his indigenous culture and he was
conditioned to a specific musical tradition. Though not in
a necessarily verbalized form, he carried the elements of
this tradition over into his New World experiences. Merriam
takes this position when he says:

> We must turn here a moment to a facet of the
> problem which is of considerable importance...
> the great importance which music plays in West
> African culture. Hardly a single daily activity
> passes without music; music is of integral im-
> portance in religion; music serves as an aid to
> work; music is one of the chief means of social
> comment and criticism; West Africa is saturated
> with music. Is it possible to believe that the
> African carried this rich musical tradition to
> America unconsciously? Of course he was cons-
> cious of it in this sense; it was, after all,

his music. It was only 'unconscious' in the
sense that it was not necessarily verbalized
as to its harmonies and melodic lines in terms
of scale steps, or to its artistic values in
terms of deep discussions of what constitutes
creative activity (Merriam 1952:7).

Evidence of the arrival of African musical traits to the
New World and its persistence in varying degrees has been
documented by Courlander (1939) for Haiti, Ortiz (1952)
for Cuba, Merriam (1951) for Brazil, Kolinski (1937) for
Dutch Guiana, Waterman (1943) for Trinidad, Roberts (1926)
for Jamaica, Parrish (1942) for the southern United States,
and others.

The music of this early "shouting" tradition in United
States Negro religion is significantly different from
those almost purely African styles of religious music
described, for other New World Negroes, by Kolinski (1937)
and Merriam (1951), in that it includes more elements of
European music. However, as Herskovits points out, it is
"important to recognize that...few New World Negro songs,
whether in Guiana or Haiti or Brazil or the United States,
are without some mark of European influence" (Herskovits
1941:267). The degree of European influence found in the
music of various New World Negro populations depends upon
the historical factors that have been operative among them.
In contrast to the history of Negro in other areas of the
New World, the unique sequence of events in the history of
the United States Negro, in particular the circumstances of

continuous and close contact with a dominant culture, has
resulted in a more accelerated rate of change from a pure
African style of music and in the development of special
musical forms. For example, except in Louisiana, African
slaves in the United States were proselyted mainly by
Protestant sects, and were offered the Protestant liturgy
and creed in lieu of their indigenous religious beliefs and
practices.

It has been noted that because of greater similarities
between the ritual practices and polytheism in African
religions and the ritual procedures and hierarchy of saints
in Catholicism, opportunities for religious syncretism were
greater in those areas of the New World where the Catholic
religion was dominant (Herskovits 1936a:635-43). Due to this
particular acculturative situation in the United States,
which also included restrictions on all-Negro religious services and the use of drums, the process of reinterpretation
has resulted in different forms of religious song than those
found, for example, in Haiti and Brazil (Herskovits 1937b,
1944) where full-blown African cults and a wide range of
African-type percussion instruments are to be found. While
the style of sacred music found in this early period among
United States Negroes is a special form, to the anthropologist "it seems reasonably clear that the idiom of which it
is a part derives from both Europe and African influences
and that something distinctive has emerged" (Merriam 1955:1174).

The lack of opportunity to retain their indigenous
musical tradition, in contrast to Negroes in other parts
of the New World, clearly did not result in the complete
loss of all vestiges of African musical values and atti-
tudes by early United States Negroes. Waterman, in a
recent discussion of African influence on music in the
New World (Waterman 1952:211-14) cites four of the five
basic characteristics fundamental to African music as being
also characteristic of United States Negro religious music.
These five basic features are: (1) metronome sense, (2)
off-beat phrasing of melodic accents, (3) dominance of percussion, (4) overlapping call-and-response pattern, and
(5) polymeter. However, Waterman states, "In the United
States Negro musical styles one of the main African components, polymeter, is usually absent except by implication...
percussion effects are stressed even in the absence of
actual instruments....The overlapping call-and-response and
the off-beat phrasing of melodic accents are important features of the religious music of the United States Negro and
a well-developed metronome sense is required for its appreciation" (Waterman 1952:216). Herskovits, in speaking of
generalized characteristics of Negro music, earlier cited
other correspondences, in addition to citing the call and
response pattern: (1) the close integration between song
and dance, (2) the cultural importance of improvisation,
and (3) the relationship of the melody to an accompanying

rhythm (Herskovits 1941:265).

Many nineteenth century observers took notice of the
unique style of music that developed as a part of the
"shouting" tradition in the United States Negro religion.
Their references, scattered in various types of literature,
form a body of information from which insights into specific
aspects of this early style, as well as an awareness of such
matters as instability of text and form, and classification
of song types, can be acquired.

The most important aspect of the style is rhythm. A
compelling necessity for it is shown by the customary hand-
slapping, foot-tapping, and overt motor behavior of singers,
which indicates the close relation between song and dance.
While the emphasis on rhythm seems especially important in
songs used for dancing (religious dance), the marking of
basic rhythm by some kind of body movement is noted even in
non-dance music (Barton 1899a:717). Thus, singers, while not
actually performing a dance, generally marked the rhythm with
swaying motions of the body and kept time with their hands
and feet (Forten 1864:589).

Closely associated with these strong rhythmic aspects
of the music is the overlapping call-and-response pattern.
As commonly conceived, the pattern is an alternation of song
phrases by leader and chorus, or chorus and chorus, or choir
and congregation; this manner of responsive singing is well
established. In this style, however, an overlapping takes

place wherein the leader starts his phrase before the chorus
phrase is completed, and often, the ending of the leader
phrase is overlapped by the chorus. An example of this pattern is taken from an early description of slave singing:

> ...the leading singer starts the words of each
> verse, often improvising, and the others, who
> 'base' him, as it is called strike in with the
> refrain or even join in the solo when the words
> are familiar. When the 'base' begins the leader
> often stops leaving the rest of the words to be
> guessed at, or it may be they are taken up by
> one of the singers. And the 'basers' themselves
> seem to follow their own whim, beginning when
> they please and leaving off when they please
> (Allen, Ware, and Garrison 1867:v).

The importance of this call-and-response pattern and its
relation to the metric framework for some kind of body
movement is indicated in the descriptions of the use of song
with various activities. Kemble points out the relation
of the pattern to the rhythm of oar strokes wherein the
sound of the oarlocks is used as rhythmic accompaniment to
song (Kemble 1863:218). Olmstead, in describing a burial
scene, tells of the body bending and motions of the song
leader and the heavy response of the chorus "in the manner
of sailors heaving at the windlass" during the filling of
a grave (Olmstead 1904:II,28). Barton gives details of the
singing of construction gangs wherein the call-and-response
pattern set the timing "to which spades sink into the clay
or the picks descend" (Barton 1899a:708).

Rhythm was expressed in the various series of regular
pulsations, in units of two, three, or four, which con-

trolled the leader-chorus phrasing and body motion. However,
a further expression of rhythm came in the unique arrangements of accented and unaccented melodic pulsations. These
irregularities of rhythm, which fall between the down and
up-beats and usually anticipate the expected or normal pul-
sation, keep up a compelling sense of movement and form a
component of Waterman's concept of "hot rhythm" in Negro
music (Waterman 1948:3-16). In recognizing this element
in the early style, Baton cited it as a kind of syncopation:

> The burden of the song is the response 'Death
> goner lay his cold icy hand on me'. An inde-
> scribable effect is given to the 'cold icy
> hand' by a syncopation. The word cold has the
> accent on the downward beat, and the first
> syllable of 'icy' takes a half note in the
> middle of the measure (Barton 1899b:448).

The term syncopation has reference to the stressing in
melodic rhythm a normally unaccented or weak beat. In this
style, however, sequences of notes (melodic phrases) are frequently shifted from the normally emphasized beat either in
advance of or behind it. As Waterman states: "...in terms
of total musical effect this label syncopation is felt to
be misleading and the more cumbersome but more general designation off-beat phrasing of melodic accents is preferred..."
(Waterman 1952:217).

In addition to the "off-beat phrasing" other melodic
peculiarities are characteristic of the style. The wide
use of graces (slurs, portamento, appoggiatura) in conjunction with certain emotional extremes expressed by dis-

tinctive vocal qualities, produced rare auditory experiences
for early observers. The music contained what were regarded
by unaccustomed ears as uncertain tonalities and rhythmic
irregularities eliciting descriptions as "wild and barbarous...
but not without plaintive melody" (Olmstead 1904:II,28),
"employing drawling intonations" (Seward 1872:29), and using
"tortuous quavers" (Murphy 1899:661).

When these musical "crudities" were investigated beyond
the level of listening, the student met with complications,
for it was difficult, if not impossible to reproduce these
sounds effectively in terms of conventional musical language
and symbols (Fenner 1878:preface). The common opinion was
that the delicate shading and variations in pitch used by
singers could not be reproduced on paper at all, and thus
the early observers and collectors sacrificed accuracy of
reproduction in the hope of preserving at least a reasonable
facsimile of the early songs for posterity. Those who
lacked the technical ability necessary for notational transcription, such as Macrae, Olmstead, and Higginson, made only
verbal references to the music.

In this early style, harmony, as conceived in the music
of Western culture, was felt by some observers to be lacking,
and the opinion was also expressed that there was no part
singing in the Western sense, although there seemed to be
harmony. Barton attributes the presence of "harmony" in

the early style to independent melodic variation among the
singers. In speaking of a song to illustrate his point he
says:

> In theory the song is sung in unison and there is
> no proper harmony. But in practice the more inde-
> pendent singers introduce grace notes and slurs,
> and the higher and lower voices range above and
> below in fifths and thirds in the more descriptive
> portions... (Barton 1899a:717).

There are other references to this problem, but it is difficult to determine whether the writers refer to the precision of individual vocal lines in a polyphonic sense, or
the coincidence of vocal parts, in a homophonic style, to
form chord patterns intentionally. Olmstead, for example,
speaks of both independent parts and perfect harmony:

> The common plantation negroes or deck hands of
> the steamboats will often in rolling cotton
> bales or carrying wood on board the boat fall
> to singing, each taking a different part and
> carrying it on with great spirit and inde-
> pendence and in perfect harmony as I never
> heard singers who had been considerably edu-
> cated at the North (Olmstead 1904:II,195).

The Reverend William Malet speaks of harmony in his description of the music he heard, but further indicates the
independence of vocal parts by referring to performances
as "regular fugues":

> ...both men's and women's voices mingled in soft
> though far sounding harmony...sometimes they
> sent forth regular 'fugues' (Malet 1862:49).

There is no reason, however, to discount completely the
references to the use of harmony, since it has been pointed

out that the musical styles found in Africa include both
harmonizing and non-harmonizing varieties (Waterman 1952:
207-209), and thus the use of harmony was not foreign to all
the slaves. However, in the case of the New World Negro
idiom, the presence or absence of harmony seems to depend
upon the point of view of the observer. If the individual
voices are considered as independent and equally important
melodies the style may be considered polyphonic. If, however,
the emphasis is seen to be placed upon a single voice or
melodic line accompanied by other voices which fill an
auxiliary function, then the style may be considered predominantly harmonic in character. Significantly enough,
there is certain emphasis on one voice in the leader part of
the call-and-response pattern, and yet in the chorus response which serves an auxiliary function in the total song
structure the harmony does appear to be created by independent
melodic variations. Thus, it appears that the kind of "proper"
harmony and part singing in the strict homophonic style of
Western culture was not a characteristic of the early style
of Negro religious music.

The music of this early period was a new manifestation,
and as such, individual songs could be expected to yield a
variety of forms and expressions based upon the fundamental
musical character of the tradition. The fusion of African
musical idioms with those of Euroamerican culture under

varying conditions seems to have precluded strict uniformity
of musical design among all slaves in all places and to
have given the tradition on the whole a conspicuously fluid
quality. To be sure, there was communication between slaves
in various states as evidenced by the practice of selling and
trading slaves, as well as the movement of slaves with their
owners, but regional differences both between and within the
upper and lower South, for example, have persisted, as shown
by differing versions of particular songs found in various
localities. For example, in tracing the song "O'er the
Crossing," the words sung to one tune in Caroline County,
Virginia, were sung in Augusta, Georgia, to the tune of "My
Body Rock Long Fever" which was collected in Tennessee
(Allen, Ware, and Garrison 1867:72). Kilham cites this
interchange of words and tunes as occurring during a single
session of singing by a group. Some hymns, especially the
favored ones, were sung several times in the course of a
religious service, each time to a different tune, and where
the text and the tune were in different meters, word sylla-
bles were either extended, often over many beats, or con-
tracted to fit the shorter meter of the tune (Kilham 1870:
309).

Not only was there variation in the fitting together
of words and music, but in words to words as well. Favorite
chorus phrases were found in association with verses to which

they apparently had little or no relation and thus, to the outsider, the songs seemed to be a patchwork of poetry in which incongruous meanings and sentiments were joined together in an attempt by uneducated slaves to create poetry (King 1875:609). Kilham cites several examples of phrases which she felt were put together without "the slightest perception of any incongruity" (Kilham 1870:309).

> The colored people scarcely ever sing a hymn without a chorus, their favorite being "Shall we know each other there?" This they sing with almost everything. Sometimes with rather startling association as:
>
> (leader) Plunged in a gulf of dark despair
> (chorus) Shall we know each other there?
> or:
> (leader) Hark from the tombs a doleful sound
> (chorus) Shall we know each other there?
> or this which is one of the most popular:
> (leader) Hell is a dark and drefful affair
>   An' ef I was a sinner. I couldn' go dar.
> (chorus) Shall we know each other there?

This "patchwork of poetry" stems from the fact that verses were not standardized as to order, nor did they belong strictly to any particular song. The non-standardization of song verse was the function of a tradition in which individuals were singled out because they possessed certain musical talents. As in the African musical tradition (F.S. Herskovits 1935:95) a good memory for, and facility with, both words and tunes, as well as improvisation, were important elements; a song leader had to be one who could improvise spontaneously.[1] The congruity of verse lines and

[1]This tradition has close resemblance to the Dahomean pattern in which "the singer who introduces new lines to

chorus depended upon the ability of the leader to improvise
with taste and skill. While the matching of verse and
chorus almost at random led to some odd combinations, the
results were generally found to be in good taste when the
songs were led by an able and experienced leader (Barton
1899b:452). Some of these leaders, as Barton points out,
when approached outside of the singing situation could
recall but few lines of verse, but in the act of song worship
they "not only remember them by the score but...fit together
words from different sources without a second's reflection"
(Barton 1899b:452).

The matter of content is closely related to that of
form, for it is in the way in which verse and chorus are put
together that song form is determined. Many of the early
songs were constructed from meager material in which verse and
chorus were in simple short-phrase, call-and-response form;
"a strict parallel with African songs" (Johnson 1944:128).
An example of these short-phrase songs is "Show Me the Way":

```
(leader) O my good Lord,
(chorus) Show me the way,
(leader) O my good Lord,
(chorus) Show me the Way,
(leader) O my good Lord,
(chorus) Show me the way,
(all)    Enter the chariot, travel along,
(leader) Noah sent out a mourning dove,
(chorus) Enter the chariot, travel along,
(leader) Which brought back a token of
```

songs has the esteem of his group" (F. S. Herskovits;
1935:95).

                  heavenly love,
(chorus)   Enter the chariot, travel along
                  (repeat A section and end)

Some are found to have emphasis on the chorus response and

a development of longer phrases:

(chorus) Little David, play on your harp,
           Hallelu, hallelu,
           Little David, play on your harp,
           Hallelu.
(leader) Little David was a shepherd boy,
           He killed Goliath an' shouted for joy.
(chorus) (As before and end)

Still others combine the short-phrase, call-and-response

pattern with a long-phrase choral refrain which dominates

the entire song:

(leader) Not my brother, not my sister,
           But it's me, O Lord,
(chorus) Standin' in the need of prayer,
(leader) Not my brother, not my sister,
           but it's me, O Lord
(chorus) Standin' in the need of prayer.
(chorus) It's me, it's me, it's me, O Lord,
           Standin' in the need of prayer,
           It's me, it's me, it's me, O Lord,
           Standin' in the need of prayer.

Regardless of type, a number of variations were possible

through the repetition of various parts, and thus sections

of a song could be extended at the whim of leaders or by

local custom. Two patterns of repetition which show dis-

tinct local custom in matters of form have been cited

(Allen, Ware, and Garrison 1867:xxii). At Fort Royal, South

Carolina, the custom was to repeat the verse of a song as

many as a dozen times before going to the chorus, which was

also subject to numerous repetitions. The usual practice in

Virginia was simply to repeat the chorus twice after each
verse. The signal for repetition was the injection of such
expressions as "I say now," or "God say you must" (Ibid.).
As may be noted, even in the simplest form (short-phrase)
the A and B sections are identifiable and, as entities, are
subject to repetition.

Religion was of great significance to the early Negro[1]
and had an apparent influence upon the secular aspects of
his culture. Bruce points out that his religious concern
was not restricted by time or place, but was carried into
every situation and activity (Bruce 1899:94). This condition had a definite impact upon musical culture as shown by
the fact that, except for funeral chants, there appears to
have been no strict designation for the sacred or secular
use of most religious songs. Depending upon local custom,
many of the same songs used for shouting (religious dance)
were also used while rowing boats, marching, doing plantation work, and so on. However, characteristics of songs
showed a corresponding change according to the activity
with which they were used.

> On the water oars dip 'Poor Rosy' (a spiritual)
> to an even andante; a stout boy and girl at the
> hominy mill will make the same 'Poor Rosy' fly
> to keep up with the whirling stone...One woman,
> said to me: 'Pshaw ...dese yer chil'en, dey
> just rattles it off...it can't be sung wid out

[1]For a full discussion and documenation of this point
see: (M. S. Herskovits, 1958:207-213).

a full heart and a troubled sperrit....!(Allen,
Ware and Garrison 1867:xxii).

The melodic phrasing of songs was also noted to change in

character:

> The same songs are used for rowing as for
> shouting...I think the hold on 'Oh in Rain-
> fall' was only used in rowing. When used as
> a shout I am quite sure that it occupied only
> one measure....One noticeable thing about
> their boat songs was that they seemed often
> to be sung just a trifle behind time; in
> 'Rainfall', 'believer cry holy' would seem
> to occupy more than its share of the stroke,
> the 'holy' being prolonged till the very
> beginning of the next stroke...(Ibid.,xv).

In addition to the use of religious songs with secular

activity, the interplay of religious and secular aspects

of culture seems to have resulted in a class of songs

which could be viewed on the one hand as religious songs

showing such apparent secular influence that "one often

detects the profane cropping out, and revealing the secular

origin" (Allen, Ware and Garrison 1867:vii), and on the

other, as songs of apparent secular origin and usage to which

the pervading influence of religion has given "a religious

echo" (Bruce 1899:94). Such songs did not reveal this

quality to the casual observer, and thus Higginson, in his

efforts to study the creation of religious songs, was per-

plexed by his informant's demonstration of a religious song

about "de ole nigger-driver" (Higginson 1870:197). His

dilemma stemmed from failure to recognize the fact that all

songs classified as spirituals were not strictly religious,

showing instead a blend of secular and religious interest.

As Johnson phrased it:

> ...although the Spirituals in general classifi-
> cation fall under the heading religious songs,
> all of them are by no means religious in a
> narrow sense. All of them are by no means songs
> of worship...(Johnson 1926:12).

Three songs of this apparent blending are found in an
early collection:

I. 1. Done wid driber's dribin's, (three times)
        Roll Jordan Roll.
    2. Done wid Mars's hollerin', (three times)
        Roll Jordan Roll
    3. Done wid Missus scoldin', (three times)

II. 1. I saw de beam in my sisters (or name of a
        person) eyes, Can't saw
        de beam in mine;
        You'd better lef' your sister door,
        Go keep your own door clean
    2. And I had a mighty battle like-a
        Jacob and de angel, Jacob, time of old;
        I didn't tend to lef' em go
        Till Jesus bless my soul.

III. (chorus)
        Nobody knows de trouble I've had,
        Nobody knows but Jesus,
        Nobody knows de trouble I've had,
        Glory hallelu'.
    1. One morning I was a-walking down,
        O yes, Lord',
        I saw some berries a-hanging down,
        O yes Lord'. (chorus)
    2. I pick de berry and I suck de juice,
        O yes, Lord'.
        Just as sweet as the honey in de comb
        O yes, Lord'. (Repeat chorus and end)
        (Allen, Ware, Garrison 1867:songs 59,
        23,74)

The blending of religious interest or meaning into
some work songs or topical songs complicates matters, so
that outside of the observed function (the setting in which

which a song is found) and obvious word meaning, classification by an informant is the sole criterion for distinction
between religious and secular song. This dynamic quality of
musical tradition, expressed by the sometimes confusing creations of its carriers, makes it difficult for the student
to establish precise terminology or to set up clear-cut types
for classification. The early religious songs have been
variously identified in the literature as: spirituals,
jubilees, shouts, funeral chants, and song narrative (also
railroad song) (Barton 1899a:707), but it is difficult to
distinguish one from another with any degree of precision.
The shout, for example, could be any of the other forms when
its function is changed from a non-dance to a dance song.
The classification of a song as a shout[1] ("running spiritual"),
or spiritual, then, is variable, and since in various localities certain favorite songs were chosen for shouting purposes,
classification also depends upon local custom. As one work
stated:

> The shouting may be to any tune and perhaps all
> of the songs are occasionally used for this
> purpose....In practice, however, a distinction
> is generally observed. The first seven...favorite
> hymns in St. Helena, Church, would rarely if ever,
> be used for shouting; while probably on each
> plantation there is a special set in common use
> (Allen, Ware, Garrison 1867:xv).

[1]The shout is a religious dance usually performed in
a circle though solo performances have been cited (Parrish,
1942:34). In the ring-shout the dancers move counter-
clockwise in a shuffling step. A group of singers stands
aside and provides the music and hand-clapping.

It is important to note that a lively tempo was not always
used, since the shout step was known to vary with the
tempo and character of the song. Some of the shouting has
even been described as "rather solemn and impressive"
(Forten 1864:589), although most historical references
describe it as hysterical and frenzied, and present day
observations also reveal a preponderance of a lively
kind of physical activity.

In addition to the sub-classification of religious
songs as dance (shout) or non-dance (other types), distinctions were sometimes made according to mood, as in the
case of the spiritual and jubilee. Songs of a sad or
solemn nature were called spirituals, "a song of sorrow"
(Morris 1956), or "a song of sadness born out of a real
condition" (Dorsey 1956). As one New Orleans jazzman
phrased it, "the spiritual is most like a blues ballad in
the style of, say, (Billy) Eckstine or (Arthur) Prysock"
(Fontenette 1955). The term "spiritual" seems to have
been used because of the relationship between this type of
song and the "spirit" or "holy spirit." As expressed by
an old slave on Avery Island, Louisiana:

> De spirituals cums from yo' spirit an' goes to
> de spirit an' yo' spirit praises de Lord
> (McIllhenny 1910:30).

Another old slave in Kentucky gave a similar explanation:

> ...in de ole days dey call 'em spirituals 'cause
> de Holy Spirit done revealed 'em to 'em (Murphy
> 1899:661).

Because of its solemn nature, the spiritual was used
for "moanin"--"dese spirituals am de best moanin' music in
de world..."--which is a solemn rite engaged in by individuals seeking to "get religion and be saved" (Ibid.).
As described in early times:

> Preachers used to get up and preach and call
> moaners up to the moaner's bench. They would
> all kneel down and sometimes they would lie
> down on the floor and the christians would
> sing...moaners would come up for two and three
> nights waiting to feel something or hear some-
> thing (Fisk University (1934:48).

The music used was solemn and pleading in character
as the moaners sought signs of being saved. But when they
"came through" and the moanin' was over the mood changed to
a happy one. They would get to "rolling and shouting and
tell everybody that they had found Jesus and they would
shout and shout" (Fisk University 1934:48).

Songs of this happy or rejoicing mood were called
jubilees. The jubilee is said to come from the heart of
the individual, as opposed to the "Holy Spirit," causing
him to sing to God of his happiness (McIllhenny 1910:30).
The jubilee is a song of praise, as is the spiritual, but
it is jubilant rather than sad (Dorsey 1956). Because of
the more frequent use of this lively type of song for
religious dancing (shout), the terms "jubilee" and "shout"
tended to be used synonymously[1], and W. C. Handy showed

[1]Present day informants tend to use the terms in
this way.

this when he distinguished the "lively shout songs" from the spirituals (Scarborough 1925:271).

Songs for the dead (those sung at funerals, burials, and wakes) are surely of the spiritual type, as distinguished by mood; thus songs such as "Lay This Body Down" were sung at the night funerals so characteristic of Negro slaves (Rogers 1867:47), and similar songs were sung during the custom of "sittin' up" with the dead.

> These midnight wails are very solemn to me....
> I have known the negroes to get together in
> groups of six or eight around a small fire and
> sing and pray alternately from nine o'clock
> till three the next morning, after the death
> of one of their number (Allen, Ware, Garrison
> 1867:19).

Music used for burials was also solemn in nature and is frequently described as having a "doleful" sound supported by "moanful rhythm" (Showers 1898:481). Though some of these songs may have begun as Western hymns, they soon slipped into the traditional pattern of Negro music described by more than one observer as being "confused chants":

> Another man...stepped into the place he had
> first occupied at the head of the grave; an
> old negro with a very singularly distorted
> face, who raised a hymn which soon became a
> confused chant...the leader singing a few
> words alone and the company making a response
> to them...The music was wild and barbarous
> but not without a plaintive melody (Olmstead
> 1904:II,26).

In the funeral custom of some Negroes a form of dance (marching) around the coffin is part of the ritual, and this indicates the employment of a spiritual type of shout song in some cases.

> When a pater-familias dies his family assemble in the room where the coffin is, and ranging themselves around the body in the order of age and relationship, sing this hymn ("These are my Father's Children"), marching round and round. They also take the youngest and pass him first over and then under the coffin. Then two men take the coffin on the shoulders and carry it on the run to the grave (Allen, Ware, Garrison 1867:101).

The song-narrative, as the term implies, is a form of story-telling; its inclusion in the religious category is justified by the use of themes from scripture. Songs of this type were free in form and created without the distinct purpose of making a song. There was probably no special ending, since the songs could be stopped with the refrain at any time or extended at the whim of the leader. Described as "long drawn, monotonous chants," they were characterized by the half-sung, half-spoken style of the leader, in which the singer employs a limited melodic range, while the chorus makes irregular contributions of ejaculations and refrain.

Used in the church services the song-narrative was led by the preacher, as a song-sermon; the congregation, with intermittent expressions of "amen" and "yes, Lord" acted as the chorus. Its use has been cited for the custom of sitting up with the dead (Barton 1899a:101), where it was employed after the repertory of regular songs had been exhausted. As well as appearing in a religious setting, the song-narrative was performed by large groups of workers with a lead singer. As used by railroad workers:

> The songs require little expenditure of breath...
> the refrain comes at considerable and irregular
> intervals, just often enough to quicken the
> lagging interest of any who may have dropped out.
> Only the leader attempts to sing the words, though
> perhaps a few nearest him catch a strain here and
> there; but the tune, which often runs along for a
> dozen verses between la and do, is hummed by others
> far and near, and gives the time to which the
> spades sink into the clay or the picks descend
> (Ibid.).

In brief summary, it is important to point out that the musical performances of this early period were congregational in nature; that is, although there was a song leader, general participation in the singing was the rule. The only special groups of singers were those who performed for dancers in the ring-shout. As has been noted, rhythm was the most important element in the style, as revealed not only in the close relation between song and dance but in the expression of basic rhythm by hand-clapping and foot-tapping, and in the distinctiveness of melodic rhythm as expressed in "off-beat phrasing." Melody, in addition to off-beat phrasing, was distinctive in its melodic ornamentation and variations in pitch that frequently occurred. Also included in the melodic aspect was the distinctive overlapping call-and-response pattern. Harmony was present but not in the strict sense of Western homophonic music;

rather it was achieved as the result of independent melodic variations in chorus phrases.

As might be expected of a tradition in its formative process, even under the most favorable circumstances the degree of standardization to be found is much less than that in a long standing tradition; thus, the matter of interchanging words and music in this early period may be viewed without undue alarm. The non-standardization of words themselves, however, is another matter, which arises from an earlier tradition in which improvisation was of primary concern to the Negro's indigenous African culture.

Finally, in the matter of classification, by combining the criteria of function (in terms of dance and non-dance) and mood, three recognizable major types and special types are to be derived:

1. Spiritual--a song that is sad in mood.

2. Jubilee--a song that is happy in mood.

3. Shout--a song used for dancing that may be of either a spiritual or jubilee type.

A. Moanin' Song--a special song of the spiritual type.

B. Songs for the Dead--special songs of the spiritual type.

C. Song Narrative--special type song with combining features: Shout-jubilee or shout-spiritual depending upon usage.

III. THE MIDDLE PERIOD

1. Regional Setting

In the post-Civil War period most Negroes remained in the Southern rural regions. Although they theoretically had greater freedom of movement, there was no significant migration during this period, either to the recently opened West or to the North. Explanation of this relative geographical stability has posed a problem for students (Myrdal 1944:185). Lack of capital and an apparent decision of white settlers in the West to use Mexican and Chinese labor are partial explanations for the failure of the large-scale migration of Negroes to that area. The anticipated rush of Negroes to Northern states also failed to materialize, presumably because of the labor monopoly of European immigrants and the fear of strange surroundings in the North; prior indications of their desire to remain in the South were noted by various observers:

> At Beaufort, South Carolina,
> ...except in rare instances, there is no disposition to go North. As long as life can be made even tolerable to them in the South they prefer to stay in their homes (Hooper 1863:4).

> At Craney Island, Virginia,
> They do not desire to go North...I have several times tried to find house servants willing to go with the prospect of a permanent home and good wages but always have difficulty in finding those willing to go (Brown 1863:6).

48.

At Helena, Arkansas,
> In the event of emancipation there would be no
> disposition to go North. Emancipation fully
> carried out and secured they would nearly all
> much prefer to live in the South (Sayer 1863:7).

Of some six and a half million Negroes in the total
United States population in 1860 approximately six million
resided in the South (U.S. Bureau of the Census 1945:
Series B, 48-71), and ten years later, ninety-nine percent
of the seven and a half million Negroes were living there
(U.S. Bureau of the Census 1910:175). Approximately twenty-
one percent of the Southern Negroes were classified as
urban dwellers, while in the North the Negro population included some sixty-nine percent urban dwellers. The census
of 1910 showed little change in the overall regional residence of Negroes; however, while the rural-urban population
in the South remained substantially the same, in the North
the urban Negro population increased approximately ten
percent (U.S. Bureau of the Census 1910:II,175). Thus, from
the end of the Civil War to the first decade of the twentieth
century Negroes tended to remain in the South where they
had always been concentrated, but at the same time there
was a definite trend toward urban living as shown by an
increase of the total urban Negro population from 9.8 percent in 1890 to 27.4 percent in 1910. In fact, the urbanization of the Negro was increasing at a more rapid rate than
that of the white population:

That the Negro population in our large cities is
increasing with greater rapidity than the white
population appears clearly when the totals of the
two races are obtained for the 38 cities, each
of which had at least 100,000 inhabitants in 1900.
The increase of Negroes in these cities, 1890 to
1900, was 38.0 percent and that of whites was
32.4 percent, and in the five Southern cities
of this class, Baltimore, Washington, Louisville,
Memphis and New Orleans, the whites increase was
20.8 percent...Growth of the white population in
the South has been almost as rapid in the country
districts as in the cities...the Negro population
is increasing in Southern cities about one-third
faster than in country districts (Stone 1908:
481-83).

2. Education

Prior to the end of the Civil War, educational opportunities for Negroes were practically non-existent, and
indeed, the act of teaching Negroes to read and write was
considered criminal and prohibited by laws passed in many
Southern states (Reed 1914:191). As a result, only a
comparatively small proportion of the mass of emancipated
Negroes was acquainted with the rudiments of primary education. The United States census of 1870 shows that five
years after freedom eight percent of the Negro population
over ten years could not write, (U.S. Bureau of the Census
1870:396-97), and that, further, only 180,372 out of a
total population of more than four million Negroes were
recorded as attending school (Ibid.).

Education for Negroes in these early years after
Emancipation was gained largely through the instruction
and funds provided by missionary societies from the North,

such as the Freedmen's Aid Societies of Boston, New York
and Philadelphia (New York Daily Tribune 1867:2). As a
result of an acute need for teachers, Negroes who had
even limited education were pressed into teaching service,
often those "whom a little while before did not know one
letter from the other" (Marsh 1892:11). Thus, Maggie L.
Porter (an ex-slave and Fisk Jubilee Singer) who began
school at the age of twelve was qualified two years later
by the Board of Education in Tennessee to teach in one of
the rude log cabins provided for the public instruction of
Negroes (Ibid.).

In response to the urgent need for Negro teachers the
Bureau for Freedmen, Refugees and Abandoned Lands (Freedmen's
Bureau), as well as various religious denominations, established schools and colleges at which Negroes received
training and education. Though most of these schools were
called colleges and universities, instruction in the early
years was on an elementary level. Completion of a full
college course was uncommon, not only because of the difficulty of students in paying the costs, but also because their
lack of previous training required a lengthy period of
preparatory education before college courses could be mastered.
Many of those who graduated from the college level took as
long as ten years to do so: Georgia Gordon (one of the
original Fisk Jubilee Singers), for example, entered Fisk

in 1866 and did not qualify for the Freshman class until
1872 (Marsh 1892:110).

There was little general interest in the problem of
Negro education among responsible civil authorities in the
Southern states. Although there had been a free school
system for white children before the Civil War, the addition of Negro children to the school population after
Emancipation demanded greatly increased expenditures for
public education. The increased taxation necessary to meet
such a financial burden, in addition to the continued belief in the Negro's inferior learning capacity, made the
free school system in the South highly unpopular among
whites (New York Daily Tribune 1867:2). Fortunately some
Northern industrialists began to show concern for this
problem and made moves to stimulate interest among Southern
communities for meeting their responsibilities for public
education. Support came mainly at the beginning of the
twentieth century from such organizations as the General
Education Fund (1903), the Jeanes Fund (1905,) and the
Phelps Stokes Fund (1910), whose influence in developing
public schools for Negroes throughout the South was considerable.

3. Social Classes

The United States Negro population in pre-Emancipation
times was, of course, characterized by a large majority

of slaves[1] in various conditions of servitude and of varied experience in the ways of the dominant culture, but, buttressed by a smaller number of free Negroes, this segment of the population already showed the beginnings of class structure. After Emancipation, social stratification among this group was more varied in character. Such factors as denial of opportunity for learning, economic gain, and freedom of movement, as well as social isolation, were no longer such formidable barriers for increasing numbers of individuals eager to improve their status, and in those areas where time and historical circumstance had served to mitigate former conditions, the Negro social structures began to exhibit levels that corresponded to those of the upper, middle, and lower levels of the white group.

Negroes in Southern rural areas were the largest in number and formed the bulk of the lower classes. In terms of economic gain and cultural change, they were less effected by Emancipation than upper and middle class Negroes of the urban North and South, retaining a lower standard of education and economic life, and showing less inclination toward

[1]	1790	1800	1810	1820
Slave:	697,681	893,602	1,141,362	1,538,022
Free:	59,527	108,435	186,496	233,634
	1830	1840	1850	1860
Slave:	2,009,043	2,487,043	3,204,313	3,953,760
Free:	318,599	386,293	434,495	488,070

(U.S. Bureau of the Census, Historical Statistics of the United States, 1789-1945 Series B 48-71.)

the customs and values of the dominant culture (Brackett
1890:372; Robinson 1889a:697). In many respects, the pattern of living found among these ex-slaves was but little
changed from that of pre-Civil War days. They lived in
the same crude one- and two-room cabins (New York Daily
Tribune 1869:2), and followed the same coarse diet (Nordhoff
1876:70); they continued their patterns of recreational
song and dance and tradition of African type folk-tales
(Bradley 1878:67; Flemming 1905:24); their characteristic
religious beliefs and customs were greatly in evidence
(Blacknall 1883:682; Stearnes 1872:348); and their religious
activities, which were restricted and often practiced in
secret during slavery, were now intensified and more
frequent (Stillman 1879:120; Avary 1906:203-4).

Although some rural Negroes managed to purchase land
and farm for themselves, the majority were almost completely
dependent upon the large plantation owner for their daily
living; the economic relationships between the Negro and
the plantation owner were of three general types. The most
common was sharecropping, the second, land renting, and the
third, wage labor (New York Daily Tribune 1870:2). In the
share system the cropper worked the land, planted, culti-
vated, and harvested the crop, while the land owner provided
him with land, implements, and supplies. The harvested
crop was divided equally between the cropper and the land

owner. In the system of land renting the rental was usually
a fixed sum per acre which varied from year to year with
the current crop price and the character of the soil.

The wage laborer was paid either a fixed monthly sum
or by the task; in the former case he also received daily
rations of food:

> The wages paid on large plantations are very small
> compared to our northern rate. The able-bodied
> men get eight dollars per month and...rations of
> one-half pound of bacon and two pounds of meal
> daily, for each hand, besides the rent of the
> cabin. The women get four, five and six dollars
> according to working ability with rations. The
> daily rations are valued at ten cents, and are
> served only to the laborer and not to his family
> (Stetson 1877:26).

The task system was derived from slavery times when a
slave's work was laid out in tasks or half acres (Anon
1872b:22). The worker lived on the plantation and was allowed to raise a food crop for himself and his family:

> Mr. B. has over two thousand negroes scattered
> over fifty thousand acres of land, and each
> family has almost unlimited choice of a spot
> upon which to settle. To clear a space and
> build a log-hut chinked with mud takes but a
> short time...each one can cultivate all the
> rice he wishes upon the land set apart for the
> purpose and there are hundreds of acres of
> woodland through which his hogs may roam and
> from which he cuts his fuel...the workers
> earn fifty cents a task...the foremen of the
> gangs are paid by the day, at a higher rate,
> the wages vary according to ability and rank
> (Ibid.).

To insure a profit or payment of rent (payment usually
in the product) (Stetson 1877:26), the labor and progress

of planting and harvesting done by the cropper, renter, or
wage laborer was supervised. Both cropper and renter were
generally under white supervision (Stone 1908:99), but:

> ...the supervision over a renter is not as
> strict as that over a cropper, and as soon as
> his account is paid his cotton is at his own
> disposal. More privileges and a large measure
> of independence are considered by the Negro as
> incident to this tenure and as he becomes the
> owner of a mule it is his ambition to become
> a renter (Ibid.).

The wage laborer was under closest supervision. Not
only was there a general supervisor of labor, usually the
planter, but the labor force was divided into gangs headed
by foremen.

In contrast, numbers of Negroes in the towns and cities
were more fortunate in terms of education and economics and
were more inclined toward the patterns and values of the
dominant culture. These urban Negroes showed stratification
into lower, middle, and upper classes; and thus in Maryland:
"Colored society has rules as strict as the laws of the
Medes and Persians. It is full of circles and each succeed-
ing circle holds itself proudly above the one just below it"
(New York Times 1887:12). Robinson (1889b:639) took note
of the social stratification that existed among Negroes in
the District of Columbia during the late nineteenth century,
citing the existence of three classes based upon certain
cultural and economic criteria:

> There are to be seen every one of the many phases
> of negro life. Some of them live squalidly in

miserable cabins or shanties, and crowded into
them in such large numbers as to seem more like
bees in a hive than human beings. Others in
better circumstances have comfortable houses,
are well clothed, and are apparently quite
prosperous. Then, again, there is the still
higher class, who live in fine houses, and
surround themselves with all the luxuries and
refinements of life. They dress in the latest
style, attend the influential churches, frequent the concert, lecture and theatre, and
in every way seem to be quite the equals of
white people (Ibid.).

Similar stratification was noted by Turner (1911:139) for

Philadelphia, and Brackett (1890:372) for the Negroes in

Baltimore.

The upper classes were usually composed of those who

were highly motivated toward white upper class patterns of

behavior (Robinson 1889b:689). Professional people (medi-

cine, law, the ministry, and so on), as well as other

economically well-to-do and educated persons, were included

in this class, and as a social group they set themselves

apart from the general Negro population. A description of

this class in Philadelphia was given by Turner who noted

that they:

Had lectures, literary societies, and Demos-
thenean institutes for both men and women; and
that they had among them ministers, physicians,
and at least one artist. These negroes of pro-
fession along with other well-to-do colored
people formed a society large enough to be
divided into numerous distinct circles...they
were hospitable, they visited frequently; and
they entertained in well furnished parlors
with music and refreshments (Turner 1911-139).

The middle classes consisted of persons with similar

cultural orientation but lesser economic means who had
taken advantage of opportunities for education and training
in various trades: barbers, carpenters, caterers, small
merchants, and the like. The members of both upper and
middle classes were among the descendants of those members
of the free Negro population or the small part of the slave
population who enjoyed educational and economic advantages
and were orientated toward urban living prior to Emancipation
(Birnie 1927:17-20; Russell 1913:14).

The lower classes of the cities and towns included
those who were perhaps less ambitious and certainly less
educated and less successful economically (Turner 1911:142),
and their failure to accept fully the values and patterns
of the dominant culture tended to set them apart. The
existence of this class was obvious to contemporary observers, not only because of their numbers, but because of the
sharp contrast between their behavior and that of others
whose "ways of living and acting and general characteristics
(were) so similar to those of their white fellow citizens
as to excite no comment whatever" (Robinson 1889b:689). This
class was formed mainly of the bulk of the southern rural
Negroes who came to the cities of the southern and border
states during and after the Civil War. Other than the
possession of freedom, their social, cultural, and economic
condition was but little changed from that of slavery times.

As in the rural setting they dwelt in one room cabins which
were almost completely without furniture except perhaps for
a rude bed, a table, and a few stools. The cabin itself,
as during slavery, was built of pine logs or rough boards,
and was roofed with shingles (New York Daily Tribune 1881:3);
they were in sharp contrast to the dwellings of upper and
middle class Negroes:

> Every Southern town is belted around with a zone
> of negro dwellings...some comfortable little
> cottages with gardens belonging to the former
> class and others wretched hovels where the latter
> class huddle together...(New York Daily Tribune
> 1877:8).

Like their rural counterparts, members of the urban lower
classes retained the customs of pre-Civil War days (Turner
1911:142; Brackett 1890:372).

4. Patterns of Religious Expression

Prior to the Civil War, the common church service patterns for Negroes were: (1) the mixed church, in which
Negroes were restricted to the galleries or other special
parts of the church, and (2) the separate church where special
services for Negroes were presided over by white ministers.
The all-Negro church was less common in the South than in
the North and was generally found among free Negroes. Where
a Negro minister was allowed to preside at meetings for
slaves he was closely supervised: "The old master would
read the Negro parson a chapter in the Bible, select his
text, and give him some instructions about handling the

subject" (Cade 1935:327). In this, and other ways, Negroes were greatly restricted in their religious activities.

Emancipation, however, removed the external pressures, and Negroes were released from the galleries of the white churches, were no longer required to have passes in order to go to the church, were not restricted as to day or time of worship, were able to choose their own ministers who could preach as they wished, and were able to worship as they pleased without fear of disturbing the master or attracting the patrols assigned to break up unauthorized all-Negro congregations. As had occurred among free Negroes and those few slaves who enjoyed relative freedom during pre-Emancipation days, the emancipated mass of Negroes now formed their own denominational churches, often with the aid of the white religious bodies whose galleries the Negroes had formerly occupied (Jordan 1905:599). Negro Baptist churches in the South maintained some association with white churches of that denomination until about 1880 when they formed a convention of their own (Dubois 1903:178), while the Negro Methodists of the North had formed independent associations much earlier.

In the course of fifteen years after Emancipation (1880) the all-Negro church became the dominant organization, and churches which were exclusively Negro were credited with over eighty percent of the Negro church-going population

(U.S. Bureau of the Census 1915:51). The majority of these
church organizations were Baptist; next largest in number
were the Methodists, and greatly in the minority were the
Presbyterians and Episcopalians (Ibid.).

TABLE 1. Negro communicants by denomination

Denomination	Organizations(%)	Members(%)
Baptist	53.4	50.4
African Methodist Episcopal	10.6	16.9
African Methodist Episcopal Zion	7.3	13.1
Colored Methodist Episcopal	1.4	0.7
Presbyterian	1.0	0.6
Episcopalian	0.2	0.3

Efforts of the Presbyterian and Episcopal churches to
establish Negro churches through missionary work met with
little success, and further, the galleries of the white
churches of these denominations were not but little used by
Negroes (Blacknall 1883:683). The culturally conservative
ex-slaves tended to follow their previous religious choices,
and previously the Presbyterian and Episcopal churches had
attracted "very intelligent" Negroes and those less conservative elements that considered themselves the better class
(Jackson 1931:199). The Presbyterian church as described
by one observer, was not popular among the large majority
of lower class Negroes:

The Presbyterian church has never had a very
large following amongst the colored people.
This is not due to a lack of interest on our
part...Indeed, in former days we were foremost
in efforts to awaken a general interest on their
behalf. We had encouraging success in this
work, in gathering a goodly number of them into
our churches, where they were trained as intelligent christians. Some of this class still clings
to us, and belong to the very best grade of their
people, intellectually and morally (Stillman 1879:
126).

On the other hand, the Baptist and Negro Methodist churches

held great appeal for the masses of Negroes even before

Emancipation; and because their doctrine and ritual were

"incomprehensible and therefore repellant to the Negroes"

(Blacknall 1883:683), the Presbyterian and Episcopal churches

in the South found it difficult to hold their Negro members

if they had opportunity to affiliate with the Baptist and

Negro Methodists (Reed 1914:190).

The religion of the Negro slave was characterized by

emotional prayers and appeals to the Deity, and abundance

of music (mostly original songs), a vehement and impassioned

style of preaching, and religious dancing and the phenomenon

of possession which frequently resulted from the intense

mental and emotional stimulation of worship. After

Emancipation there was a general revival and growth of this

"old-time" religion. Released from restrictions on reli-

gious activity, Negroes held worship services with greater

frequency than in the past, and often extended them beyond

ordinary periods of time (Stillman 1879:120); meetings

which in the past were limited to a few hours were now extended for weeks and even months, and behavior was intensely emotional, since there were no longer restrictions
of quietness with which to contend. The excitement, shouting, and dancing could often be heard at great distance
(Avary 1906:203-04), and observers in separate parts of the
South took notice of the persistence and growth of this
religion among the freedmen:

> At Helena, Arkansas:
> The religious element exists to much larger
> extent evidently than among whites. They are
> exceeding susceptible to religious emotions.
> They have a number of their preachers here,
> and many meetings, greatly thronged and long
> continued (Fitch 1863:9).

> At Fortress Monroe, Virginia:
> Their religious element is marked and strong,
> though crude, partaking largely of the
> relics of heathenism and slavery. One
> thing is clear, while their old habits
> and customs cling to them in their modes
> of worship, their faith and confidence in
> Divine revelation is prominent and univer-
> sal. Meetings are kept up nearly every
> evening in the week and have been for months
> (Wilder 1863:5).

The attraction of the majority of Negroes to the
Baptist and Methodist faiths, rather than to other denominations, was related to the particular patterns of worship.
The relatively dull services found in the Presbyterian
and Episcopal churches lacked appeal for the majority of
Negroes. As one Presbyterian observed: "Our characteristics as a denomination are not popular with the masses

of Negro people. Our quiet, instructional method of preaching our orderly worship, the simplicity of our forms and the terms of membership...are distasteful to them" (Stillman 1879:126). The religious customs of the Baptists and Methodists, on the other hand, allowed opportunity for types of religious behavior and practice fundamental to the religious aspect of United States Negro culture.[1]

The practice of religious dancing, the style of preaching, and the customs of possession and type of baptism found among United States Negroes deviated greatly from the standards of practice and behavior found in the Presbyterian and Episcopal churches. The religious dancing of the Negroes, variously termed "shout," "holy dance," and "walk into Egypt," involved a circle formation using a shuffle step with body motions which complemented the rhythm of the dance in a jerking fashion; dancing was usually accompanied by a group of singers who stood aside and marked the rhythm by hand-clapping or striking other parts of the body (Spaulding 1863:196-8). Such behavior could scarcely be considered compatible with the requirements of "quiet, orderly worship" demanded by the Presbyterian and Episcopal denominations.

The moans, shouts, jumping, stamping, and dancing created

[1]This is also characteristic of the United States Negro's pre-American patterns of worship.

an emotional atmosphere conducive to the phenomenon of
possession[1] without which "shouting" services were regarded
as a failure (Macrae 1870:I,70). Barton's account of a
"shouting" service describes how the fervor generated resulted in various manifestations of state of trance (possession) among members of a congregation:

> The company has long been swaying back and forth
> in the rhythm of the preacher's chant, and now and
> then there has come a shout of assent to the oft
> repeated text. Each time the preacher's almost
> incoherent talk become articulate in a shout, 'I
> have trod de wine-press,' there are cries of 'Yes!,'
> 'Praise de Lawd' and 'Glory' from the Amen corner,
> where sit the 'praying brethern,' and from the
> Hallelujah corner, where sit the 'agonizing sistern.'
> In the earlier demonstration the men rather lead, but
> from the time when Aunt Melinda cries out, 'Nebbah
> mind de white folks,' 'My soul's happy,' 'Hallelujah,'
> and leaps into the air, the men are left behind.
> Women go off into trances, roll under benches, or go
> spinning down the aisle with eyes closed and with
> arms out-stretched. Each shout of the preacher is
> a signal for someone else to start; and, strange
> to say, though there are two posts in the aisle,
> and the women go spinning down like tops, I never
> saw one strike a post...I have seen an old man stand
> in the aisle and jump eighty-nine times after I
> began to count, and without moving a muscle of his
> thin, parchment face, and without disturbing the
> meeting (Barton 1899b:41-42).

The method of baptism favored by the majority of Negroes

[1]The phenomenon of possession accompanied by dancing
and singing is an outstanding feature of religious expression among African and New World Negroes. Comparison
of the outer forms of possession as found among United
States Negroes indicates a retention of the old form of
expression through the mechanism of reinterpretation. This
is particularly evident in the similarity of patterns of
motor behavior and in the social aspect wherein possession
occurs as a part of the religious experience of the group.
For a full discussion of the point see: (M.J.Herskovits,
1958:209-265).

Negroes was immersion in water as opposed to the sprinkling
on of water practiced by the Presbyterians and Episcopalians.
For the Negroes, immersion was fundamental (Stillman 1879:
120), and the "only authentic and efficacious mode of
baptism" (Blacknall 1883:681), and was not only comprehen-
sible in terms of their cultural past (Herskovits 1941:
232-34) but seems to have had an equal importance in the
acculturative situation. The ceremonies, which took place
at almost any accessible body of water, were important occasions which attracted large crowds; great attention was
paid to detail:

> The ceremonial of baptism is peculiar and consists
> of preliminary services in the church. A procession
> is then formed, headed by the pastor, who is fol-
> lowed by the converts, all in emblematic white robes
> and white cotton gloves, the congregation bringing
> up the rear, singing psalms and hymns and spiritual
> songs through the streets to the town to the banks
> of the river. There after prayer, exhortation and
> more singing they are dipped in the muddy water, and
> struggle out through the yellow slimy mud, shouting
> in religious frenzy 'Glory to God'. In the afternoon
> all again repair to the church, the converts dressed
> in 'ball costume' and bridal array, to hear more
> preaching, and join in congratulations and singing.
> This is kept up until evening, with gradually increas-
> ing fervor until the climax of the holy dance
> (Stetson 1877:9-10).

And finally, an additional indication of the importance of
the ritual of baptism is seen in the custom of rebaptizing,
especially when changing to a new church (Flemming 1905:273).

Successful growth of the "old-time" religion was due
in large part to the satisfaction of the emotional needs of

Negro congregations by Negro ministers who knew what kind of
religion their people wanted and were capable of providing
it. Though most of the Negro ministers were illiterate,[1]
they possessed a style of oratory which swayed their eager
and sympathetic audiences, and by the sheer repetition of
simple phrases and showy gestures they were able to arouse
their congregations to states of religious ecstasy. Brown
describes the effect of this style of preaching as he observed it in a church in Nashville, Tennessee, in 1880:

> A large assembly was in attendance, and a young
> man from Cincinnati was introduced by the
> pastor as the preacher for the time being. He
> evidently felt that to set a congregation to
> shouting was the highest point to be attained
> and he was equal to the occasion. Failing to
> raise a good shout by a reasonable amount of
> exertion he took from his pocket a letter, opened
> it, held it up and began, 'when you reach the
> other world you'll be hunting for your mother,
> and the angel will read from this paper.'...For
> fully ten minutes the preacher walked the pul-
> pit repeating in a loud incoherent manner,
> 'and the angel will read from this letter.'
> This created the wildest excitement, and not
> less than ten or fifteen were shouting in dif-
> ferent parts of the house, while four or five were
> going from seat to seat shaking hands...The
> pastor highly complimented the effort as one
> of 'great power', which the audience most cor-
> dially endorsed (Brown 1880:192-3).

The concentration of Negroes in the rural South meant
that the religion which developed among them was that of a

[1]"The great majority of Negro preachers of the South
are extremely ignorant. Many of them we are assured by the
best testimony do not know enough of the gospel to lead
a poor inquiring sinner to Jesus Christ or salvation"
Baptist Home Mission Monthly, (August 1878,p.19).

predominantly uneducated, culturally conservative group.
The presence, especially in urban areas, of elements in
the Negro population which were less conservative and
which had the advantage of education and training in the
ways of the dominant culture gave rise to a different type
of all-Negro church. Thus all-Negro religious organizations were broadly separated into two types distinguished
by the kind of leadership and the pattern of worship.

The most common religious type was that found among
rural Southern and lower class Negroes in the cities
and towns; its salient features have been described above.
The Baptist minister exercised independent and almost absolute control over his church; his power was...great, almost
boundless. Within his own parish he was practically priest
and pope (Blacknall 1883:685). Since Baptist churches were
independent of any governing body, almost any group of four
or more members could organize a church under an ordained
minister. Ordination in this denomination, however, was
not difficult, since the only requirement was the "call
to preach"; the ability to read and write was of little
or no importance (Jackson 1931:199). The Methodists, on
the other hand, established a centralized government and
made it more difficult for a man to become a minister, or
for new churches to be established, and this fact seems to
be responsible for the preponderance of Baptist churches.

As summarized by one student:

> It was a decidedly easy matter for Negro Baptist
> churches...to split and thus multiply. While
> the Methodists might hesitate to establish an
> additional church so close to another...the
> Baptists in the heat of controversial excitement
> often established two or three churches where
> there were not at first enough people to sustain
> one (Woodson 1921:25).

Greatly in opposition to the "shouting" church was
the all-Negro church controlled by educated leadership;
while they were often of the same denomination as the
"shouting" church (Negro Baptists and Methodists) their
services were more conventional (McLean 1903:67). Here
the patterns of worship closely followed those found in
the white churches, and, contrasting such a church with
the "shouting" church, it has been characterized as: "one
presided over by an educated minister with lofty ideals
and correct standards, and to whose better nature the old
order is repulsive" (Reed 1914:201).

The membership of such "progressive" churches was
composed of the educated upper and middle class Negroes
who rejected the "shouting" church for the more intellectual sermons of educated clergymen and the custom of
solemn worship services, but despite this Negro class,
a clergyman who studied the situation in the South in the
1900's noted:

> The improvement of the four-fifths of the Negro
> population who live in the rural regions is
> often exaggerated. It is still shadowed with an

ignorance which has barely been touched by the
light of the scanty school training for a few
weeks of the year and with a church life pecu-
liarly infiltrated with superstition. In vast
plantation populations the old slave church
still stands (Reed 1914:203).

Thus it seems clear that there were comparatively few
of the "progressive" churches during this period while
the demand for "shouting" churches was large.

There is evidence that the older order in Negro
religion began to be challenged in the latter part of this
period by educated Negro ministers who endeavored to change
the customs of "shouting" congregations:

Among the colored people, there have been movements
toward wholesome changes in the large colored
churches. The value of many of the old features
of religious life is more and more called in
question. The old-time 'shout', the frenzy which
fastened upon one who 'got religion' are passing
away as the old-time plantation has passed away.
All the ministers present at a district conference
of the African Methodist Episcopal Church in 1887,
voted for a resolution offered by one of the present
young clergy of Baltimore, that camp meetings and
bush-meetings, as carried on among their people
were not productive of sufficient good to make
amends for the evil effects they had on the churches.
These views are not yet universal and are held more
in city than in country, but the whole body of the
churches must become gradually touched by the
leaven of education (Brackett 1890:390).

However, change from the old order was by no means common
among "shouting" congregations where adherents of the old
tradition were prone to leave a church or eliminate the
pastor if the services were not to their taste. Because of
this conservatism in religious matters, many ministers were
of necessity forced to follow old traditions:

...the educated minister will often preach
unseen and waste his eloquence on the desert
air. He soon finds that not only is his
church losing its pristine prominence, not
only is his own reputation as a representative
clergy waning, but that there is soon a very
perceptible diminution in the loaves and
fishes. It is a problem, and is forcing young
preachers who would otherwise do good work in
the ministry into the old ruts which while their
better natures condemn it, they have not the
power to resist (Reed 1914:201).

5. Patterns of Religious Musical Expression

As we have seen, the majority of the United States
Negro population in the post-Civil War period was made
up of ex-slaves who tended to remain in a southern rural
setting, to be conservative in their cultural outlook and
to continue in the "shouting" religious tradition of which
their music was an integral part. There was also present
in the total Negro population a minority more susceptible
to change in the direction of the patterns of the dominant
culture, including the religious aspect of culture and its
concomitant musical traditions as well. In this period,
then, there existed two Negro religious music traditions:
(1) the new tradition developed among educated upper and
middle class Negroes, and (2) the old, perpetuated by the
larger body of lower class individuals.

A. The New Tradition

The new tradition in Negro religious music began among
Negroes at various schools established for them after the
Civil War, and notable among the various groups which arose

was the student choir trained at Fisk University in Nashville, Tennessee. It was here that the new trend began and from here that it diffused.

The student choir at Fisk was developed by the school treasurer, George L. White, who also conducted singing classes at the institution. White chose the most promising voices, gave them special training, and formed them into a choir; after annual concerts beginning in 1867 he presented the group in the seventeenth century cantata "Esther" before a large audience of whites in Nashville, and, encouraged by his local success, he took part of the choir to other cities in the state of Tennessee.

Stimulated by growing popularity in the state, White decided to organize a small student choir which could travel through the North and raise funds for Fisk, and thus, with a group of eleven students, six women and five men, he started the first tour from Nashville on October 6, 1871. At first the group had no name, but a month later White decided to call it the "Jubilee Singers," a name chosen from an Old Testament phrase "year of Jubilee" which had become a popular figure of speech among the slaves in referring to the time when they would be emancipated. Since the choir was not singing slave songs at this time, the choice may have been suggested to White by the fact that all but two of the singers were ex-slaves.

It was not until the singers reached New York City that
slave-songs came to be dominant in their repertory. Here-
tofore they had featured classical renditions of Christian
hymns and such popular songs as "Home Sweet Home" and "Old
Folks at Home," but at the close of a Friday evening prayer-
meeting in the church of Reverend Henry Ward Beecher, they
sang some slave-hymns and were launched on the road to
international fame, scoring great successes in New England,
Great Britain, and on the European continent, as well as
in the United States.

In addition to presenting the slave songs internationally,
the Fisk group, and those who trained them, played a very
significant role in fostering a new tradition in Negro
religious music, for the Fisk influence served as a counter-
force against an inclination to abandon the old tradition
in Negro religious music. At this time there existed a strong
tendency, especially among the educated elements in the
Negro population, to revolt against any former customs connected with slavery, including the slave songs. Thus Haskell
reported:

> As the Negro becomes educated he relinquishes
> these half-barbaric, but beautiful old words
> and melodies, and their place is taken by the
> denominational hymns and the Moody and Sankey
> songs which are more and more popular where-
> ever schools have sprung up (Haskell 1899:377).

The trend toward avoidance of the folk-hymns in favor
of denominational songs was more pronounced among the younger

generation attending the schools (many of whom had not been slaves or had only a slight recollection of slavery) than among the older generation of ex-slaves (Macrae 1870:68). The disdain of the latter for those who relinquished the old tradition is expressed in the comment of a former slave: "Dese young heads ain't wuth killin'; for they don't keer 'bout de Bible nor de ol' hymns...de Big organ and de eddication had done took all de Holy Spirit outen 'em" (Murphy 1899:66).

Prior to the appearance of Negro folk-hymns in their repertory, the Fisk Singers had followed the trend away from the old music tradition, but their ultimate fame rested upon their performances of the folk-hymns and the highly popular publications of these harmonized "Jubilee songs," as their versions were commonly termed. The success of this group in gaining recognition from the whites prompted a reappraisal of the value of the old songs on the part of those Negroes who had turned away from them, and this aroused consciousness was also stimulated by the high degree of financial success achieved by the Fisk Singers. At any rate, the changed attitude was marked by the outcropping at Hampton, Tuskegee, Atlanta, and other Negro schools, of choral organizations dedicated to the preservation and development of the old slave hymns.

In addition to affecting choirs at other Negro schools, the Fisk group also influenced the development of independent

singing groups. Such professional groups were no longer
connected with educational institutions, although they
used the term "Jubilee" in their titles and drew their
membership partly, at least, from school choirs. For example,
after George L. White gave up the management of the Fisk
group in 1882, several independent groups rose in competition for the market in Negro religious song performances,
each bearing the words "Fisk Jubilee Singers" in their
titles; groups from other school choirs did likewise. Thus,
a second result of the "Fisk Trend" was that it set a pattern for the development of Negro groups which performed
hymns for a listening audience; these songs in their natural
setting were essentially congregational in nature and relied
upon audience participation for their performance.

Of further importance in the development of Negro sacred
song in this period was the influence performing groups had
on untrained as well as trained or educated Negroes. Membership in the splinter groups noted above was drawn from
the educated and uneducated alike, and something of a premium was placed upon the less educated as sources of original
songs to add to the group repertory. Barton underscores
this point:

> Not very long ago I attended a concert given by
> a troupe of jubilee singers whose leader was a
> member of the original Fisk company. Toward the
> end of the programme he announced that a recently
> arrived singer in his troupe from Mississippi
> had brought a song that her grandparent sang

in slave times which he counted the saddest and
most beautiful of the songs of slavery (Barton
1899a:609).

Barton also makes a distinction between educated and uneducated jubilee singing groups. While he does not cite any
differences in musical styles of these musically trained and
untrained singers, his reference to "companies of educated
jubilee singers" (Ibid.,617) does indicate the existence of
groups of Negro singers influenced by the Fisk trend and
yet whose members were untrained musically.

A specific difference between the trained and the untrained singing group was doubtless the marked influence
of European values in music, a hallmark of the educated
singers such as comprised the Fisk group. Indeed, the
strict discipline to which the Fisk Singers were subjected
in their university studies, and the substantial training
and instruction in the European system of music they received
was quite effective in changing their musical values.
Critical observers found the music of the Fisk group to be
in style too refined to genuinely represent the Negro musical
style (Seward 1872:3). In explanation of their musical
style Theodore F. Seward, the first to put these songs on
paper and to harmonize them for publication, pointed out
that in addition to being educated in the European tradition, the Fisk Singers "also received considerable musical
instruction and (had) modified their manner of execution"

(Seward 1872:29). He further pointed out that their education had caused them to abandon the usual Negro dialects and to eliminate the custom of marking rhythm with body motions, the use of graces, sliding intonation, and certain other rhythmic and melodic irregularities common to the original style of music (Ibid.).

Thomas P. Fenner, who worked with Negro students at Hampton, summarized the dilemma faced by proponents of the school of academic Negro music when he wrote: "There are evidently...two legitimate methods of treating this music: either to render it in its absolutely rude simplicity, or to develop it without destroying its original characteristics; the only proper field for such development being in the harmony" (Fenner 1874:172). He further pointed out the difficulty of writing the melodic lines as sung in the folk tradition, and, indeed, in written versions not only were the melodic lines sheared of their characteristic graces, slurs, and other "crudities," but the harmonic concept was altered as well. As Barton (1899b:449) points out: "In the published Jubilee songs, the harmony has been added for piano and quartette; but it is rarely found in Negro songs" (Ibid.).

A final important point is that the trend begun at Fisk influenced the development of the art form of Negro sacred song. This art form is represented by the arrangements for trained choirs by such respected Negro musicians

as John Work of Fisk, R. Nathaniel Dett of Hampton, Clarence
Cameron White of Hampton, and the solo arrangements of the
famous singers Harry T. Burleigh and Roland Hayes. Possibly
influenced by the Romantic movement dominant in the European music at the time, such educated musicians, by the
modification of folk peculiarities and the incorporation of
elements from the European music tradition, developed art
forms of Negro folk music. The melodic lines of the songs
written in this style are polished and refined, and the graces
and slurs found in the folk-song sources omitted. While
harmonic simplicity is maintained, the art form accedes to
the demands of the European music tradition in the use of
strict four-part harmony in choral versions. The position
of the vocal parts, in terms of the prevailing chord structure, is strictly prescribed, accompaniment is optional, and
many choirs peform in the a cappella style of the folk idiom.
The solo songs, however, are generally sung to the accompaniment, almost invariably of the piano, though songs are oc-
casionally scored for voice and orchestra. The accompaniment
is used as rhythmic support for a song or, by the use of the
harmonic coloring of sustained chords, to create the mood
dictated by the meaning of the verse.

Most of the songs are the strophic type and follow
closely the original forms of the folk versions which include
the short-phrase, call-and-response, the long-phrase call-

and-response, or a combination of short-phrase call-and-
response, with a long-phrase choral refrain. The choral
versions of the art form include a call-and-response
pattern, often with a solo voice taking the place of the
leader's phrase found in the folk idiom, although in many
arrangements, different vocal parts (i.e. tenor or soprano)
are assigned to the leader phrases. Further, overlapping
of normal leader-chorus phrases does not always occur in the
performances of the trained choir, and definite breaks
between the solo and chorus parts are either written into
the music or demanded by the conductor.

       B. The Old Tradition

    Through a recognition of shared experiences, the majority
of enslaved Negroes created a way of life which, while influenced by Euroamerican culture, was distinctive. The
religious tradition of this New World Negro culture was
vital and "deeply integrated into the daily round" (Herskovits 1941:207), and following Emancipation, there was further expansion of religious activity and a prodigious increase in the number of all-Negro churches where the practices
of the bush-church could now be freely enjoyed. The old
music style was an integral part of this religious tradition,
and thus, while some Negroes tended to discard the more
distinctive elements of the old style of religious music
as "relics of degredation" (Anon 1914:611), to Negroes who
held fast to the "old-time" religion the old style of music

was still vital and meaningful.

Although adherence to the old tradition was most wide-
spread in the rural districts of the South, the "old-time"
religion and its concomitant musical tradition was also
found in the large cities and in areas where schools had
been maintained for some time (Anon 1890:82). The prevalence
of religious dancing, exhorting sermons and prayers, and
characteristic music were reported by more than one observer whose comments showing the prominence of music in
church services (used for dancing, in various rituals, and
even during sermons) indicate the continued importance of
the old style of music. Thus one observer noted:

> And now commenced a religious dance, perfectly
> indescribable, and as long as I have been in
> the South it was perfectly new to me. The
> leader started down one of the aisles chanting
> a weird plantation song, and every joint in
> his body moving in time with the measure; the
> sisters took it up and followed two by two
> until there was a complete circle all around
> the church, all dancing in time with the music.
> We were told that they would keep this up until
> morning...All through the pastor's exhortation
> the audience were keeping up a sort of rhythmic
> accompaniment with body and intonations...(Ibid.).

Another observer points out the persistence of the old
tradition in music and its use for ritual purposes:

> These services begin with singing, which consists
> entirely of sonorous nasal sounds. If by chance
> a semi-modern tune is chosen, it is distorted
> almost beyond recognition. In many of the churches
> the old Jubilee songs are still employed...I
> attended one Methodist Love Feast. The flock was
> told to lay aside all enmity and break bread with
> all...The bread and water were passed from one

to another, exchanging bits of bread and accompanying the exchange by a hearty hand-shake. They moved
in sort of rhythmic motion, waving to and fro as
they chanted (Bryant 1892:301).

Maclean comments on the ritual use of music in a Primitive

Baptist church early in the twentieth century:

> The service (footwashing) generally ends with a
> kind of a dance, which they call 'Rocking Daniel.'
> No information could be gained as to the origin
> of this most peculiar custom. A leader stands in
> the center of a circle, which the members form
> in front of the pulpit. They begin with singing
> the lines 'Rock Daniel, Rock Daniel, Rock Daniel,
> till I die'. Gradually they move round in the
> circle, single file then begin to clap hands
> and fall into a regular step or motion which is
> hard to describe. Finally, when they have become
> worked up to a high state of excitement, and
> almost exhausted the leader gives the signal,
> and they disperse...The songs sung by the church
> are extremely interesting, as they embody so many
> strange and original sentiments. These people
> seem to believe thoroughly in a noisy religion.
> They frequently interrupt the speaker with shouts
> of approval or disapproval and songs. The prayers
> are long and earnest in the extreme (Maclean 1903:
> 67).

Some innovations are found in the old tradition during

this period, including the introduction of the special

singing groups among untrained Negroes as previously men-

tioned. Another innovation was the custom of "lining off"

the hymns found in regular church hymnals. Here each line

of a song was first stated by the preacher in sing-song

fashion, then repeated by the congregation. The congre-

gational repeat was at a slow tempo and extended phrases

which included individual embellishment and interpretation

of the melody. As one informant described the style:

"People just felt as to when to release a phrase and to go up
and down with the melody. There was no director. It just
came natural. As for melody, everybody just added his own"
(M. Jackson 1958). The overlapping of individual phrases
and the coincidence of the notes of individual melodic lines
and embellishments led to the incidental creation of harmony
by the group as a whole. This rendition of hymns, which has
a counterpart in the Euroamerican music tradition, was
probably made necessary by the lack of hymnals and the high
rate of illiteracy, and was referred to as "long meter."
Since most of the hymns sung in this style were those of
Isaac Watts (spirituals and jubilees were not treated in
this fashion) the performance of them was also referred to
as "Dr. Watts."

These innovations had relatively little effect upon the
old musical tradition, and congregational singing, as opposed
to special groups, was the rule rather than the exception.
Further, "Dr. Watts" or "long meter" fitted readily into the
leader-chorus pattern of the old tradition. As indicated by
observers, the old spirituals, shouts, and jubilees[1] were

[1]In this period the term "jubilee," due to the reputation of the Fisk Singers and their publications of "Jubilee
Songs" took on an additional meaning, and was now used in
reference to the entire class of Negro religious folk-songs.
However, among the folk the old association of the term with
emotions of joy and excitement is seen in the use of "jubilee"
in reference to physical reactions to songs of a jubilant or
excited nature: "That peculiar act known as 'beating Juba'
or 'Jubilee' accompanies the singing of hymns. It is simply
the act of beating time with the hands on the body, head and

still dominant in the repertory of the "shouting" churches, and where hymns of the Western church were used, they were easily fitted into the style of the old tradition (Bryant 1892:301). Not only were the old songs still being used, but new songs in the old tradition were still being created, particularly by the more isolated groups of Negroes (Graham 1922:744).

The elements of style characteristic of the old tradition remained virtually unchanged. Rhythmic expression was highlighted by the "close integration of song and dance" (Herskovits 1958:265), as evidenced by statements of observers who described even "non-dance" situations as "rhythmic motion wavering to and fro as they chanted" (Bryant 1892:301), and "sort of rhythmic accompaniment with body and intonations" (Anon 1890:82). The embellishment of melodic lines noted as characteristic by Fenner in the beginning decades of the period (1874:172), and by Howard who noted a "delight in embellishments" in the final decade of the period (Howard 1919: 13), shows a continued tradition of the individual interpretation of melody which, as we shall see, has important implications for the harmonic aspect of this style.

In harmonic concept, as in the previous period, there was no awareness of chords and harmony as conceived in Western music. Though there was one predominant melody, the under-limbs. This is always done when the singer or audience get a little excited" (Robinson 1889a:59).

lying harmony was produced by what may be thought as of simultaneous and independent melodies improvised against the
melodic theme in polyphonic pattern. The performance of
songs in this style by large groups produced the effect of
"four and six and eight part harmonies" (Burlin 1919:500),
especially in the performance of "Dr. Watts" where each individual "just adds his own." It was also true of performances of the spirituals and jubilees by large groups of
Negroes who were conceived as being a chorus because of the
effect of the extemporaneous harmonies they produced. One
observer commented: "These nine hundred boys and girls...
whose chorus singing is so 'marvelous' are not divided and
seated according to 'parts' like the usual white chorus;
indeed technically speaking, this is no 'chorus' at all..."
(Ibid.). Even in attempting to write down the harmonies
used by a small group of untrained jubilee singers, Howard
found it difficult to distinguish the various parts (Howard
Q919:13), for the Western concept was not applicable. The
fact that no singer in the group was able to sing his "part"
alone led the investigator to conclude that:

> The Negroes have a decided polyphonic instinct
> and that they have inherited this from their
> African ancestors is undeniable...The instinct
> is absolutely spontaneous and the Negro has no
> more idea what chord he is helping to make than
> an infant would have. It is just because of this
> ignorance of musical notation that the spontaneity
> of their polyphony is so remarkable and in many of
> their songs it would be a difficult task indeed for

a trained musician to improve the natural beauty of their harmonic coloring (Ibid.).

A final persisting characteristic was the tradition of unaccompanied singing. While the "jubilee" versions and art forms were scored for instrumental accompaniment, instruments were never used in the folk tradition; in fact, the use of the piano and melodeon for church services was viewed as a sinful practice by adherents of the "old time" religion. As expressed by an ex-slave who had serious misgivings about Episcopalian services:

> For what with ya gittin's up and ya setting's down and ya 'sponsin' and ya prayin' prayers that a man up North made and put 'em in a book and ya mellydoriums (melodeons) a playing all ther time you's so took up the Spirit can' come nigh ya. Why, Honey, dese same old eyes is seed ya preacher lookin' on at folks dancin' and breakin' der commandments. An dat ain' all. My Polly says she seed him fingerin' de fiddle hisself, and mighty nigh about to play (Blacknall 1883:684).

Indeed, members of the Primitive Baptist church and other strict sects were not allowed to use musical instruments for any purpose. For the more pious, dancing and the singing of secular songs were viewed as unpardonable sins, and use of musical instruments associated with them was unspeakable. Blacknall makes this point quite clear in citing the case of a musician who destroyed his instrument after "getting religion."

> In the neighborhood lived a cheery, light hearted negro fiddler called 'Sol'. Sol through the rendering of divers of his pieces might have grated

somewhat on an over refined ear, saw fit to dub
himself 'er born musicaner'; and as his music
sufficed to dance by no one challenged his right
to bear the title. His position was both popular
and lucrative. In fact, the earnings of his fiddle
were about double the gross product of his little
farm...Finally there opened a revival exceptionally
long, fervid, and uproarious. Sol 'come through',
and his first act of atonement was to immolate with
all due solemnity his fiddle as both fiddle and
instrument in his old ways of unutterable turpitude
leaving its shreds as any accursed thing by the
stump over which it was shivered (Blacknall 1883:684).

However, the non-use of instruments in church did not
mean that Negroes were unfamiliar with them or with the
concept of instrumental accompaniment. It was doubtless only
the more pious devotees who strictly obeyed the edict of not
playing instruments, for, from Colonial times, Negroes had
been noted for their instrumental playing and secular dancing
(Watson 1846:344).

Fiddling and dancing were also favorite forms
of diversion for the slaves. Many of them played
the violin with such ease that numerous advertisements called attention to this talent. Polydor
Gardiner of Narragansett was famous in the section
as a fiddler and was in demand at parties and
balls. So too was Caesar, the slave fiddler of the
Reverend Johnathan Hood of East Guiliford, Connecticut, who was such an accomplished performer that
the minister used to call in the young people to
dance to his playing. Zelah a Negro of Groton,
Massachusetts, who later fought in the American
Revolution became famous in his neighborhood as
a musician (Greene 1942:244).

On Southern plantations the instrumental music of Negro performers was a prominent feature at cakewalks, candy-stews,
and corn-shuckings (Bradley 1878:67), and the instrumentalists
at such functions were held in high esteem. Barrow points

out this fact in his description of music played at a corn-
shucking in Georgia:

> The music is commonly made by a fiddler and a
> strawbeater, the fiddle being far more popular
> than the banjo, in spite of tradition to the
> contrary. The fiddler is the man of most
> importance on the ground. He always comes late,
> must have an extra share of whiskey, is the best
> dressed man in the crowd, and unless every honor
> is shown him he will not play. He will play a
> dozen different pieces, which are carefully dis-
> tinguished by name but not by tunes. The most
> skilled judge of music will be unable to detect
> any difference (Barrow 1882:878).

Instrumental music ranging from large brass and string bands
to the simple use of the harmonica was common practice among
Negroes. Robinson noted this wide range of activity:

> Almost every plantation furnishes banjo and fiddle
> players, who manipulate both instruments with
> wonderful dexterity, yet absolutely without the
> advantages of instruction. In nearly all southern
> cities are also to be found large brass and string
> bands (whose performers play by ear) conducted solely
> by negroes who are constantly engaged by whites on
> all public and festive occasions requiring the
> assistance of music...Even a simple harmonicon, or
> mouth organ, becomes in their hands a little musical
> instrument of rare melody and sweetness, and I have
> heard little half-naked darkies on the banks of the
> Southern rivers playing it, while others danced
> to its music with delight (Robinson 1898:56).

In view of the tradition of performance on musical instruments, as well as the long-established custom of using them
with singing and dancing, it seems probable that Negroes must
have been familiar with their use for accompaniment. However,
their style of accompaniment was characterized more by
rhythmic than harmonic or melodic interest, and here the

influence of the Negro's pre-American past is clearly seen,
for one of the outstanding features of the African musical system is its rhythms. As stated by Herskovits: "For the
African, the important thing about rhythm is to have it
regardless of how it is produced" (Herskovits 1950:3).
Merriam cites the ubiquity of percussive and rhythmic expression not only in terms of drumming but also in vocal
expression, melodic shapes, instrumental techniques, and
other aspects of African musical expression:

> Surely one of the characteristics of African
> music lies in its complicated fusions of various
> rhythms, and surely these rhythms are expressed
> percussively, but to see them in terms of drums
> alone is but to scratch the surface of a complex
> musical expression. For song itself, sung by
> voices or in instrumental songs, played perhaps
> on a harp, are expressed percussively and rhythmi-
> cally as well....There is no attempt here to mini-
> mize the importance of drums in much African music;
> rather, it is to point out that such a preoccupation
> is by no means exclusive, and that the percussive
> and rhythmic characteristics of African music are
> displayed throughout the entire musical system in
> terms of vocal expression, melodic shapes, into-
> nation patterns, instrumental techniques and other
> means as well as through drums and drumming
> (Merriam 1957:2).

In the case of the United States Negro the desire to
"have rhythm regardless of how it is produced" is seen in
the technique of the "straw-beater" described by Barrow
(1882:878). Here, a second musician strikes the belly of
the violin between the bow and left hand of the violinist,
with stout straws in the fashion of a drummer.

> The performer provides himself with a pair of
> straws about eighteen inches in length, and

> stout enough to stand a good smart blow. An
> experienced straw-beater will be very careful
> in selecting his straws, which he does from a
> sedge-broom...These straws are used after the
> manner of drum-sticks, that portion of the
> fiddle between the fiddler's bow and his left
> hand serving as a drum (Ibid.).

In this instance, the violin, normally a melodic instrument,
is used for percussive and rhythmic purposes, and the percussive rhythms thus produced tend to dominate the musical
accompaniment to song and dance:

> One of the first sounds which you hear on
> approaching the dancing is the tum de tum
> of the straws, and after the dance begins,
> when the shuffling of feet destroys the
> other sounds of the fiddle, this noise can
> still be heard (Ibid.).

The cultural importance of this dominant concern for
rhythm is also clearly reflected in the continued use of
drumming (Cable 1885:517; Georgia Writers Project 1940:149)
and the ubiquity of hand-clapping and foot-tapping to ac-
company religious song. The latter technique is most notable
in the custom of "basing" singers and dancers in which a
group of the best singers stands aside and sings the chorus
response while furnishing rhythm for the shouters by clapping the hands on their knees and other parts of the body
(Allen, Ware, Garrison 1867:xiv; Robinson 1898:59). The
persistence of this interest in rhythm is seen, finally,
in the unaccompanied style of untrained jubilee singers and
in the use of instruments in the religious musical style
developed in the following period.

IV. THE LATE PERIOD

Changes in Regional Setting

In the early decades of the twentieth century Negroes began to migrate from the southern rural environment which had been their home for over two centuries. The force of this migration was characterized by a "push" from the South and a "pull" from the North due to the differences in opportunities for Negroes in the two regions. The "push" in the South was generated by the infiltration of white workers into what were formerly "Negro jobs," the damaging effects the boll weevil had wrought on cotton crops, and the westward shift of cotton growing. The "pull" in the North was caused by changes in the labor market (i.e., the drafting of white workers for service during World War I and the stopping of European immigration) at a time when factories and munition plants sorely needed labor (Myrdal 1944:193). While the opportunity to improve their economic condition in the North had a strong attraction for Negroes, the desire for social improvement (i.e., better schools, social equality) was also a strong incentive for migration.

Two general northward routes were followed. It is estimated that 528,937 Negroes from Virginia, the Carolinas, Florida, and eastern Georgia migrated through Maryland and Delaware to Pennsylvania and New York, and that an almost equal number (514,550) from Alabama, Mississippi, western

Georgia, Louisiana, and Arkansas moved through Tennessee and
Kentucky to Ohio, Michigan, Indiana, and Illinois. The
population of Negroes in the South decreased during the intercensus period 1910-20 by over one million persons (U.S. Bureau
of the Census 1949:Series B48-71).

After the first World War, the trend of northward migration increased to the extent that during the intercensus
period 1920-30 the South lost approximately three million
Negroes. Of these some one and a quarter million migrated
to the North-Eastern states, another million and a half moved
to the North Central states and several hundred thousand went
westward (U.S. Bureau of the Census 1949:Series B215-230).

The northward migration of Negroes was, however, but one
facet of the total pattern. Indeed, the change in character
of the Negro population was more than a regional movement;
as Woofter suggested, "It was fundamentally a shift from country to city" (Woofter 1928:26). An outstanding feature of
this change was the tendency to concentrate in large urban
centers, both North and South, the populations of which
multiplied themselves several times during the three decades
from 1910 to 1940 (U.S. Bureau of the Census 1920:II, table 13,
14, 17; 1950:16).

TABLE 2. Negro population of selected cities, 1910-1940

	1910	1920	1940
New York, N. Y.	91,709	152,467	458,444
Chicago, Ill.	44,103	109,548	277,731
Detroit, Mich.	5,741	40,838	149,119

	1910	1920	1940
Philadelphia, Pa.	84,459	134,229	250,880
Baltimore, Md.	84,749	108,222	165,843
Washington, D.C.	94,446	109,966	187,266
St. Louis, Mo.	43,960	69,854	108,765
Memphis, Tenn.	52,305	70,230	108,938
Atlanta, Ga.	51,902	62,796	104,533

The continued "push" from the South and "pull" from the North, aided by the labor needs to support World War II and the Korean conflict, continued to attract large numbers of Negroes to the industrial centers of the North, and the Negro population in the communities of New York, Chicago, Philadelphia, and Detroit more than doubled in the decade between 1940 and 1950. The number of Negroes in each of these cities is equal to or greater than that found in many southern states; thus the Negro population of Chicago, for example, closely approximates that of the entire state of Florida and is from one to five times the number of Negroes in the states of Tennessee, Arkansas, Maryland, Kentucky, Virginia, and West Virginia respectively. The case for New York City is even more drastic (U.S. Bureau of the Census 1950:16).

TABLE 3. Negro population of selected cities, 1940-50

	1940	1950		1950
New York City	458,444	749,080	Virginia	734,211
			Florida	603,101
Chicago	277,731	586,663	Tennessee	530,603
			Arkansas	426,639
Philadelphia	250,880	480,134	Maryland	385,972
			Kentucky	201,921
Detroit	149,119	357,857	West Virginia	114,867

Educational Characteristics

The level of the educational attainment by Negroes has risen significantly along with the shift to urban dwelling and residence outside the South. Until 1940 the measure of educational status was the rate of illiteracy among a population grouping, but subsequently, the median number of school years completed came to be used as an index of measurement. The illiteracy rate of Negroes decreased from 44.5 percent in 1900 (U.S. Bureau of the Census 1930:II,1219) to 16.3 percent in 1930 (Loc. cit.). In regional differences, the South, having the largest proportion of Negroes, contained the largest number of Negro illiterates--some 93.6 percent. Approximately 43.7 percent of the rural population was illiterate, while in the urban population only 9.2 percent was illiterate; the rural population contained 76 percent of the total number of Negro illiterates.

Using the median number of school years completed as a measure of educational attainment, the last available census figures (U.S. Bureau of the Census 1950:27-30) show a higher grade level for Negroes living in urban areas of both the North and South (8.4 percent) than those living in rural areas (7.0 percent). Regionally, Negroes in the North and West had a median grade level of 8.8 while those in the South had a grade attainment level of only 6.2. Place of residence, in terms of rural or urban areas, is thus clearly

a governing factor in the educational attainment of United
States Negroes.

Occupational Characteristics

Under slavery the Negro was mainly engaged in two occupations: agriculture, and domestic and personal service.
However, since plantations were largely self-sustaining,
slave owners found it more profitable to train their slaves
in various skilled and semi-skilled trades such as bricklaying,
carpentry, blacksmithing, shoemaking, tailoring, and kindred
occupations, than to engage free white labor. Trained
Negroes were a valuable property since they were used as a
profitable source of income, not only on the plantation, but
frequently as contract labor to the public. They were
thus found in direct contact with free white labor in almost
every occupational category, and in most cases were able to
under-bid this competition for employment (Nordhoff 1865:8-10;
Phillips 1910:367-68).

Emancipation resulted in the almost immediate decline
of Negro artisans and mechanics. In open competition for
jobs, Negro skilled labor failed to gain its share of the
old jobs, or of the occupations where new techniques made
work easier and more attractive. The alternatives for
Negro workers were to continue in the recognized "Negro"
jobs which were primarily agricultural pursuits, and domestic
and personal service.

The census of 1890 showed that of Negroes ten years
of age and over, some 56 percent were engaged in agriculture
and approximately 31 percent in domestic and personal service. About 12 percent were engaged in "Negro jobs" outside
these categories, such as saw mill laborers, railroad main-
tenance men, turpentine camp laborers, porters, teamsters,
and carriage drivers. Only about one percent of these Negro
workers were found in professional service categories such
as teaching, medicine, religion, and music (U.S. Bureau of the
Census 1915:57).

Urbanization of the Negro population was accompanied by
a decrease in the numbers found in the agricultural labor
force. Between 1910 and 1920, when large numbers of Negroes
moved to the cities, the number of Negro farm laborers decreased from 54.6 percent to 44.2 percent, and as a result
of continued reductions in the rural population, the number
of farm workers represented only 36.1 percent of all Negroes
gainfully employed in 1930 (U.S. Bureau of the Census 1943:2).
With expanded non-agricultural employment opportunities in
the urban North and South, the percent of Negro farm workers
decreased to 25 percent in 1940, and by 1950 approximately
80 percent of gainfully employed Negroes were found in the
non-agricultural labor force (U.S. Bureau of the Census
1950:3B67).

TABLE 4. Changes in place of residence and size of
farm labor force among Negroes, 1890-1950.

	1890	1910	1920	1930	1940	1950
AGRICULTURE (%total Negro population)	56.6	54.6	44.2	36.1	25.7	20.5
OTHER	43.4	45.4	55.8	63.9	74.3	79.5
TOTAL	100.0	100.0	100.0	100.0	100.0	100.0
PLACE OF RESIDENCE (Rural)	80.2	72.6	66.0	56.3	51.0	34.0
(Urban)	19.8	27.4	34.0	43.7	49.0	66.0
TOTAL	100.0	100.0	100.0	100.0	100.0	100.0

(U.S. Bureau of the Census 1915:52-59; 1943:2; 1950:SB67)

Very few Negroes residing outside the South were engaged in farm labor. As late as 1940, for example, 35.2
percent of the Negro labor force in the South was engaged in
agriculture, while only 2.1 percent of Northern Negro laborers
were found in that category (Ginzberg 1956:23-28). Thus,
while the general movement of United States Negroes to urban
communities resulted in changed occupational characteristics,
their northward migration is seen to have had the greatest
effect upon change in occupation.

Social Classes and Culture Change

As has been indicated, a relatively small number of
rural Negroes drifted to the cities before the great migration.
Those who were industrious and ambitious enough to gain the
requirements of education and behavior were generally ab-
sorbed into the higher status Negro groups, but the majority

was relegated to a low status position largely because of
cultural differences from the urbanized Negroes. Since
there was a general acceptance of small settlements of
Negroes in urban communities, these early migrants, relatively few in number, caused little change either in the
size of Negro settlements, or the status of Negroes in the
cities. Although urban Negroes generally conducted a separate institutional life, in many instances they were accepted
with equality in white churches and schools, and were active
in politics (Gosnell 1935:198).

However, the sudden arrival of many thousands of rural
Southern Negroes during this period intensified the raising
of social and economic barriers between Negro and White.
Restrictions against renting or selling property to Negroes,
and discrimination against them in employment and the use
of public facilities became more rigid (Chicago Commission
on Race Relations 1922:2). The old established Negro families in the cities resented this threat to their social position and, relishing the privilege of having "long been better
off and better educated than the rest of their fellows and
better known to and (having) more to do with the whites"
(Brackett 1890:372), these families moved from the Negro
communities and isolated themselves even to the extent of
refusing to send their children to Negro public schools.

Upper class position in the Negro social hierarchy
was an ascribed social status based largely upon the factors

of white ancestry and family traditions of having been free
before Emancipation (Dodge 1886:23-30). Due to limited
employment opportunities for Negroes, occupation and income
had previously been of little consequence in determining the
status of Negro upper class members, thus, they were found in
a wide range of occupations, including teachers, physicians,
barbers, shoemakers, waiters, ministers, and blacksmiths
(DuBois 1902; Warner 1940:184ff). With the influx of large
numbers of rural southern Negroes, many of whom were for
the first time enjoying employment in the areas of skilled
and semi-skilled labor, new social distinctions, based upon
income, type of employment, and education, began to appear
among Negroes (Daniels 1914:174-83; Davis 1941:238ff). The
new emphasis on achieved social status increased social
mobility, and began to diminish the importance of family
tradition and white ancestry. In some large Negro communities,
where light complexion and Caucasian hair form had been
highly influential in determining social status, the influence
of white ancestry decreased to the point that it was no longer
necessary to "be olive, yellow or white...or even brown with
'good hair' to be a member of the upper class" (Davis 1941:247).

The nature of social stratification among Negroes, as
interpreted by a number of students (Davis 1941:238; Drake
1945:790; Dollard 1937:83), includes the conventional strata
of lower, middle, and upper classes. However, in the actual

situation there is a mixture of achieved and ascribed social statuses, and sufficient variation in class behavior to make the precise description of Negro social classes difficult. Thus, the description given here is to be regarded in general terms:

Lower Class

Term of residence:	Large proportion of recent migrants from the rural South.
Education:	High rate of illiteracy, educational attainment represents elementary school or less.
Occupation:	Some employed as semi-skilled workers, but the majority unskilled workers and laborers.
Income:	Income low and uncertain with a high percentage of public welfare cases.
Housing:	Residence largely in slum housing or public housing projects.

Middle Class

Term of residence:	Longer residence than most lower class members.
Education:	Educational attainment includes at least some high school education.
Occupation:	Wage earners in skilled and semi-skilled occupations.
Income:	Low but stable.
Housing:	Reside in standard housing often in neighborhoods that include some sub-standard lower class residences.

Upper Class

Term of residence:	Long-term residence, many with "old family" traditions.

Education: Educational attainment ranges from high school completion to some college training and degrees.

Occupation: Large proportion of professional (law, medicine, education, religion), successful businessmen and public officials.

Income: Many have incomes ranging from $20,000 to $40,000.

Housing: Well-appointed homes generally in integrated neighborhoods.

An important dimension of social class distinction among Negroes is the difference in cultural standards of behavior and value. Members of the small upper class stratum are conceived to be the most acculturated, while the middle class members are seen to be striving toward cultural assimilation and place great emphasis upon education as a means of achieving fuller participation in the national culture. The members of the large lower class are characterized not only by a low degree of adherence to American cultural standards (Myrdal 1944:701-704), but also by an apparent disinterest in achieving them; they are apparently not "dominated by mobility aspirations" (Drake 1945:789) as is the case with the middle class. Membership in the lower class is composed largely of parents and children of the southern rural migrant group whose culture "projects into the present time the attitude and behavior patterns from slavery to a great extent" (Myrdal 1944:701). Thus, the lower class stratum is distinguishable, by cultural values and standards, from the upper and middle strata, whose longer history of urban living has accelerated the effects of the acculturative process among them.

The roots of the "plantation" culture are to be found in the developments which resulted from a modification and reinterpretation of African culture under the force of the experiences of its carriers in the United States. Under the strict control of, and with economic dependency on, whites in a largely southern rural setting, the enslaved antecedents of the present-day people accommodated themselves differently to various aspects of Euroamerican culture than did the relatively smaller number of successful free Negroes and privileged slaves. A particular set of social and economic factors served to limit the degree of access to and participation in the general culture of the United States, and was important in shaping their culture; these included deficiencies in basic education, economic dependency, and occupational characteristics, and the degree and type of contact with representatives of the dominant culture.

The distinctiveness of their culture has persisted in the post-Emancipation and urban settings. Because they are unskilled workers with limited education, employment is difficult to find and, when found, is unstable; thus, their income is similarly limited, and this weak economic base has influenced many aspects of their culture. In housing, for example, the immigrant Negro population drifts to areas

of lowest rent and forms a relatively homogeneous community
that has a cultural life all its own.

> Even though the Negroes that go to cities in the
> North expect more than migrants to southern
> cities, their standards when they arrive do not
> measure up to those of the Negroes who were born
> in the North or who have lived there for some
> time. This creates a difference between migrant
> neighborhoods and well-established neighborhoods
> within northern cities (Woofter 1928:97).

In lower class Negro neighborhoods the physical character of the buildings (largely old and sub-standard) and the
distinctive cultural behavior show obvious differences from
middle and upper class Negro residential areas.

Food habits are prominently outlined by the listings and
displays in market windows which advertise yams, sugar cane,
rice, hominy grits, hog maws, chitterlings, neckbones and
other mainstays of the southern Negro diet. Countless cafes
and restaurants are found specializing in "homecooking,"
"southern cooking," and particular styles of preparation such
as Virginia, Louisiana, Georgia, and South Carolina dishes.
In true southern Negro tradition, street vendors peddle both
cooked and raw foods.

Religious customs are distinguishable on the basis of
church denominations. In contrast to the churches of
Euroamerican denomination found among the upper and middle
classes, the churches of the lowest stratum are of United
States Negro denomination, largely Baptist, Holiness, and
Spiritualist. The buildings dedicated to religion vary

widely in type, and churches are found housed in halls,
remodeled garages, vacant theaters, rooms in residences,
and store-front buildings, although a few are housed in
regular church buildings. The scores of shops dealing in
the sale of candles, oils, holy water, herbs, charms, and
kindred items indicate a considerable interest in magico-
religious practices and beliefs, frequently in connection
with church activity. Numerous signs, as well as cards and
sidewalk demonstrations, give evidence of the large body
of diviners, healers, and occult practitioners supported by
the lower class community outside regular church activity.

In this socio-cultural milieu, representatives of rural
southern Negro culture are able to identify with others
whose customs are like their own, thus gaining a sense of
belonging. Social isolation between the classes also aids
in the development of in-group solidarity, strengthens ties
to traditional culture, and hinders "adjustment" to urban
cultural value and behavior.

> Negroes who have lived in the North a long time
> look down their noses at the new arrivals. They
> crack jokes about Negroes 'fresh up from bam'
> or 'fresh up from 'sippi, fresh up from the ole
> country.' One third generation Chicago Negro
> said 'I won't live in the same neighborhood with
> those people who live like they did back on the
> plantation.' He and others like him, are the
> ones who try to move into 'better neighbor-
> hoods' (Chicago Daily News 1956:10).

During the early migration period the difficulties of
their adjustment were anticipated by those familiar with

the two cultural types:

> In considering the adjustment of the Negro
> emigrant it might be well to bear in mind this
> fact: There are two separate and distinct
> types of them, viz., the city type and the
> rural type. The rural type is by far the most
> ignorant, due to the lack of educational ad-
> vantages in the rural districts. They have
> been reared upon farms, and their work has been
> that of farm laborers. If it is true that the
> majority of the emigrants are of the rural
> type, knowing them as I do, I can appreciate
> just what a tremendous task it must and will
> be to adjust them to the environment of the
> manufacturing cities of the North and East
> (Edens 1917:511).

Forty-one years later, this anticipated clash of culture
developed into reality and became a serious problem. Citing
their cultural "poverty" as stemming from their having
"little education, little training in skills, little self-
motivation, and self-responsibility," one welfare authority
(Cohen 1958:3) has viewed the problem of their rehabilita-
tion and integration into the general culture as one that
will not be solved in the near future.

Patterns of Religious Expression

Following Emancipation, the number of independent Negro
churches was greatly increased by the large number of plantation Negroes who embraced the Negro Baptist and Methodist
denominations. The majority of these churches was southern
and rural; as late as 1936 over sixty percent of the Negro
churches were in the rural South (U.S. Bureau of the Census
1936:900), and the most common type of religious behavior

and belief was largely that which the plantation Negro had
developed in isolation from the white church. As we have
seen, not all of the religious experiences of the Negro slave
were shared or observed by their masters. Even where
Negroes were admitted into churches along with whites they
were known to have developed their own "churches" in secrecy.
As stated by one ex-slave: "The colored folks had their own
code of religion, not nearly so complicated as the white
man's religion...when we had meetings of this kind we held
them in our own way and were not interfered with by the
white folks" (Anderson 1927:22-23). Recognition of this
fact prompted one early scholar to conclude: "Under the
leadership of the priest and medicine men and afterward the
Christian pastor, the church preserved remnants of African
tribal life and became after Emancipation the center of
Negro life....The Negro church...started in the African
forest and survived slavery" (Dubois:1898 4-5).

The rural Negro church has retained a fundamentalist
doctrine. Its devotees have found no reason to doubt their
concept of an all-powerful, all-seeing God, or their deliv-
erance and salvation through Jesus Christ. They fail to
see a need for exchanging their traditional observances
and taboos for the modern practices of card playing, Sunday
recreation, and social dancing. To them God has not changed,
He is the same God that delivered and still delivers them
from "hard trials and tribulations."

This steadfast belief is nurtured and enforced by the rural minister whose power and influence over spiritual and moral life is almost absolute. Though he is usually a man with little formal education, and sometimes illiterate (Raper 1936:367; Mays 1933:238-41) he is regarded as an inspired man, one who "had a vision and heard a voice which called him to preach" (Woodson 1930:156), and who was compelled to answer this devine call "lest God might strike him dead" (Loc. cit.). Receiving his mandate from the spiritual world he rarely preaches about mundane matters such as community and social needs. Rather, his sermons stress the supernatural, the mystical, and the importance of preparing one's self in the present for the world to come. His oratory abounds with vivid descriptions of God in His beautiful heaven, the saints and angels, and the devil in the fiery depths of hell; Biblical characters and their experiences are also favorite subjects. These subjects serve as vehicles for the persistent theme of "getting religion" and "getting right with God" which run through the sermons. The oratorical style in which they are delivered is familiarly referred to as "old time" preaching; it is a rhythmical and emotional style designed to elicit responses, "arousement," and even possession (Powdermaker 1939:253-273; Pipes 1951:110-132).

Church services conducted by such a minister consist of singing, praying, and preaching while waiting for the

spirit to appear to members of the congregation. The
preacher's emotional appeal, in conjunction with the music,
evokes from members of the congregation physical manifestations of "being filled with the Spirit," shouting, dancing,
jumping, crying, and speaking in tongues (Woodson 1930:106).
Camp meetings and revival services are of the same character,
although a more intense emotional atmosphere prevails; such
meetings, which last at least a week, are designed to bring
those who are outside the "Ark of Safety" under the protec-
tion of the Almighty. The "mourner" is considered as a
candidate for membership when he convinces the elders that
he has experienced a closeness to the supernatural, i.e.,
saw a light, had a vision or a visit from Jesus, or heard
a voice; and his conversion is confirmed by the ritual of
Baptism. This characteristic religious behavior is found
among rural congregations irrespective of denomination, although the Baptists' custom of immersion in the baptismal
service is peculiar to them (Woodson 1930:152).

> Among the colored Methodists and Baptists there
> is little or no feeling of denominational dif-
> ference, members of a church which has services
> on the first and third Sundays attend some other,
> not necessarily of the same denomination, on the
> second and fourth....The unimportance of sectarian
> distinction is frequently stressed both from the
> pulpit and in conversation among the laity
> (Powdermaker 1939:233).

The majority of rural Negro churches are Baptist and
Negro Methodist, although many new denominations and inde-

pendent churches are found in the large cities. Negro
church patterns in Chicago are typical of those found in
large metropolitan areas (Drake 1945:414):

Baptist	45%
African Methodist Episcopal African Methodist Episcopal Zion Christian (formerly "Colored") Methodist Episcopal	9%
Church of God in Christ Church of God in Holiness Church of God and Saints of Christ Church of the Living God Pentecostal Assemblies	22%
Spiritualist Churches	10%
Community Churches and Independents	8%
Congregational Episcopal Methodist Episcopal	6%

The types of Negro churches are expressed even more
clearly by other characteristics. The fundamental belief
and practice of Negro congregations, in its role as a
"major focus of interest" (Herskovits 1941:207-259), has
long been the subject of much experimentation, and the
variation found in present-day Negro religious life radiates
from this core of orthodox patterns as it reflects the
degree of change or resistance to change that has occurred
among different segments of the Negro population. While
the upper and middle classes reflect greater degrees of
religious acculturation, lower class elements show a greater
degree of conservatism which is often expressed in the

intensification of orthodox Negro religious belief and
practice.

The relatively small number of upper class churchgoers
has long been associated with the Presbyterian, Congregational,
and Episcopal churches where worship is in accord with the
established practices of these "white" denominations. As
middle class members of orthodox Negro churches become more
literate and sophisticated, they demand ministers who are
educated men, sermons that are more intellectual, services
that are less emotional, and more democratic control over
church policy and finance. In some well-established churches
of the middle class (especially those of Negro Methodist
denominations), change in religious values and behavior has
reached a point where the services closely approach the
"frozen, restrained characteristics of the white church"
(Dollard 1937:246).

Less complete change is noticeable in other well-
established Negro churches where the minister is faced with
the problem of satisfying the demands of two types of communicants, adherents of the "old time" religion and the "progres-
sives." Thus his sermons do not stress only supernatural
aspects of religion, but also include something of such
worldly affairs as social and economic problems as well, and
the style of preaching vacillates between the "old time"
exhorting style and a more scholarly delivery. While

emotional response and behavior is practiced by some, it is
tolerated, but not practiced, by others.

Lower class religious values are clearly expressed in
the pattern of the small church and in the creation of new
denominations. The force of the rural tradition of small
intimate groups of worshippers has resulted in the splitting
off of groups from large congregations, and the fact that
religion represents an area of cultural focus (Herskovits
1948:542-560) has resulted in the creation of new denominations which serve as a vehicle of expression for the variations in practice and belief.

Such churches, composed of small groups of low income
individuals, are of modest means; hence, they are found in
various types of structures such as garages, houses, and
vacant stores, familiarly termed "store-front" churches. As
in the rural pattern, the concept of the "call to preach" is
primary; thus, regardless of his education or financial means,
the minister, led by divine guidance, feels compelled to
organize his church with any means available to him.

> The Negro Baptist minister who has the "call"
> feels akin to the apostle in the wilderness...
> With his Bible in his hand, and a divine sense
> of mission he rents an empty store, fashions a
> crude pulpit, buys a few discarded theatre seats
> and starts his church. He has no financial back-
> ing for his venture; in some cases his church
> may represent an investment of his life savings
> (Fukuyama 1955:12).

The minister often secures a structure that provides
both living quarters and space to be used for church services.

In some cases he secures quarters in which he can conduct
a business enterprise such as a barber shop, resale shop,
or magazine stand and, by re-arranging the furniture or
reserving a space in the rear, provides adequate facilities
for worship. As observed in New York in the 1920's (Reid
1926:274-75):

> Incredible as it may seem, there are within the
> radius of one hundred and fifty blocks of that
> section of Harlem occupied by the colored popu-
> lation, more than one hundred and forty churches.
> At the time of the count there were exactly that
> number. Since that time more have been institu-
> ted or have moved into the district. These
> churches have an estimated membership of more
> than 49,000....Only fifty-four of these churches
> are housed in regular church edifices, or resi-
> dences that have been converted to a secular
> style of architecture. The churches remaining
> are in the class known as house churches. They
> are found occupying the first floor of a private
> dwelling, a site formerly used for business
> purposes, or the back room of a flat....Rent is
> paid by the pastor or some charitable member at
> whose home the services are held, with or without
> permission of the landlord. The pastor assumes
> all responsibility for rent, light, and heat as
> well as his salary and received pro tanto all
> incoming collections.

Of the 197 Baptist churches noted in Chicago in 1955, approximately 148 were of the store-front type, and about
twenty percent of these were put to double use as living
quarters, business establishments, and churches.

One aspect of the lower class church complex in Chicago
and other urban communities is seen in the number of store-
front churches which represent splits from large churches
of Baptist denomination, or transplanted Baptist congrega-

tions from the rural South. Many of the thousands of rural migrants feel out of place in large city churches which, in addition to having more formalized services, are lacking in the warm personal atmosphere and direct communication with the pastor (who shares their interests and cultural ties) to which they are accustomed. The observing pastor of a large church often tries to create this atmosphere by devising parts of his sermon to suit their tastes and by forming clubs within the church composed of members from the same Southern communities, such as the "Greenville Club," "Abbeville Club," and the "Mississippi Club." However, more often than not, such clubs form a nucleus which either secures a pastor or chooses a leader from within the group and forms a small church of its own. In other cases, store-front churches are established by the Southern minister who has either come with his congregation or followed them to the city and re-established his church in an urban setting. In such churches the pattern of worship is almost completely unchanged from the fundamentalist doctrine and practice of the Negro rural church (Drake 1945:619-629).

A second aspect of the lower class church pattern is represented by the small groups which are completely separated from the older denominations. A dominant concern with religious form and values has often resulted in beliefs and ceremonies which are not in accord with those of the orthodox Negro church. Among the Baptists, where a long history of church splitting exists (Woodson 1921:95), the stage was set very early for the creation of new denominations, most of which were organized in the last decade of the nineteenth century. Their major beliefs and practices are practically identical:

TABLE 5. Characteristics of Holiness Churches.

	Belief	Practice
Church of the Living God (1889) (Christian Workers for Fellowship)	Repentance Regeneration Justification Sanctification Second coming of Christ	Baptism (immersion) Divine Healing Speaking in tongues Foot-washing (Use of unleavened bread and water)
Church of Christ Holiness, U.S.A. (1894)	" (Also the gift of the Holy Ghost is an act subsequent to conversion)	"
Church of God in Christ (1895)	"	"
Church of God and Saints of Christ (1896)	" (Also believe that the Negro race is descended from the ten lost tribes of Israel)	"
Fire Baptized Holiness Church of God (1898)	"	"

Belief   Practice

Church of God, Holi-
ness (1914)

(Also the gift
of the Holy Ghost

These denominations which in 1926 accounted for but
approximately one percent of the Negro churches in the United
States (U.S. Religious Bodies 1936:900), have been traditionally small in membership, but have been growing with the
rise of the urban Negro populations; in 1936 (Loc. cit.) they
accounted for approximately three percent of Negro church-
goers. There are indications that these denominations account
for a much larger percentage of Negro church-goers today, but
since many of them do not keep records, an accurate estimate
of their numbers is unobtainable. It is to be noted, however,
that the numbers of this type of church in Chicago increased
from nine in 1919 (Chicago Commission on Race Relations 1922:
445) to one hundred and seven in 1938 (Drake 1945:633). Further, the largest denomination, the Church of God in Christ,
increased its national membership from 20,805 in 1936 to
600,000 in 1951 (Ketchan 1951:59). Few of the churches number a thousand or more in their congregations; they are primarily small store-front churches, scattered through the
lower class neighborhoods, averaging sixty or less members
per church (U.S. Census of Religious Bodies 1936:900).

Because they emphasize living a perfect life free from
sin, these churches are called "holiness" or "sanctified"

115.

groups. The primary characteristics which differentiate
them from the orthodox Negro church are (1) emphasis upon
healing, (2) sanctification resulting in gifts of prophesy,
(3) speaking in unknown tongues and healing powers, (4)
shouting and the use of various musical instruments, (5)
special services called "tarrying," in which the faithful
and the mourners come to pray, testify and sing while waiting
for the "Holy Ghost" (who manifests himself in individual
behavior including running, shouting, jumping or rolling on
the floor, and speaking in unknown tongues), and,(6) contrary
to the usual pattern, the assumption of leadership by women
in the form of pastorship of churches.

A more recent denominational development among urban
Negroes is the Spiritualist church, which seems to have developed as a refinement of a complex African pattern of magic
and healing and European folk belief.

> Nothing is more common in many of the Southern
> States than for a Negro to declare himself
> bewitched, under the spell of some hurtful in-
> cantation or condemned by the evil eye to suffer
> a life of torture or to die an ignominious death.
> The case of the Reverend Barker of Clarksville,
> Tennessee, was similar to many others of the kind
> save that they do not usually prove so incurable.
> This man who had ornamented a Christian pulpit
> for many years---awoke one morning firmly impressed
> that he was 'bewitched' or 'hoodooed' as the colored
> people say, to express the malignant influence
> exercised over unfortunate beings by the voudou
> sorcerers. He was certain that a negro man whom
> he had long suspected of being his enemy had
> 'conjured' him by putting some snake bones and a
> bone from the spine of a mad dog in his hat...
> under the pressure of the hateful charms he became

hopelessly insane...The untutored, yet really imagina-
tive mind of the black has a willingness to believe in
spirits and supernatural powers and manifestations,
which render him an easy prey to designing clever
imposters of his own race...Voudouism is still practiced in Louisiana and especially in New Orleans...
probably this habit is dying out among the American
Negroes in the Gulf States; but those of mixed blood,
who have been touched but little by the schools,
and who are outside the current of progress which
has borne so many of the blacks, since the War toward
a higher life, doubtless still have a firm belief in
much that is barbaric, absurd and revolting (N.Y.
Times 1874:6).

The strong persistence of these magico-religious practices

in the rural South has been cited by Powdermaker (1939:286-

296), and indication of the migration of this tradition with

the Southern Negroes who moved to urban communities in the

North is frequently found:

...Whether they are West Indian or southern
practitioners of the occult science in Harlem,
their ritual is basically similar in form and
style to the performance of the Guinea
fetichers. They may impressively promote themselves as numerologists, magicians, oraculists,
metaphysicists or plain spiritualists. But
(it is) West Indian Obeahism and voodooism...
now transformed into mystic chapels in which
burn candles, and oils, and incense...It is not
so strange that these occult establishments
should exist in Harlem...But it is significant
that such an increasingly large number should
flourish there. Many of them advertise in
Harlem's newspapers. But the exclusive and
successful ones do not advertise. And these
constitute the majority. An indication of their
growth is the springing up of sacred shops in
Harlem. These are the depots which supply the
ritualistic paraphernalia of the occult chapels.
At first glance they appear no different from
similar establishments downtown furnishing
special religious articles for priests and
altar...But a little investigation discloses
astounding differences. Behind the pictures

and the statuary of Biblical figures...the shelves
look like a pharmacists', loaded with varicolored
jugs and euphemistic labels such as: Jupiter, King
Solomon, Felicity, Love-charm, Commander, Concentration, High John, Rosemary, Chapel Bouquet...
There are candles of every hue which are used in
the mystic rites of candle-lore. Divination is done
by the flicker of the flame or the shape of the
tallow after the wick has burned out. The color
of the candle is of special importance, as also the
day on which it should be burned (McKay 1940:74-76).

Perusal of the want-ad section of Negro newspapers

reveals numerous advertisements of practitioners of occult

science, divination, healing, voodoo, and oriental mysticism;

the Chicago Daily Defender (a Negro paper) averages fifteen

such ads per day (Fig. 1). Further evidence of the tradition

is seen not only in the special shops dealing in the sale

of candles, oils, charms, herbs, and the like (Table 6), but

also in the existence of regular drug stores in the Negro

community that carry these items for sale. While the labels

on such items sold in drug stores suggest the effects claimed

by practitioners, any claims to produce these effects are

carefully denied. For example, the Van Van produced by the

Famous Products Company of Chicago, Illinois, is advertised:

Van Van Oil is a highly perfumed oil, very strong.
Conjure Men, and so-called Voo Doos, it is said
have had great faith in a so-called Van Van Oil.
One book states that essence of Van Van is the most
popular Conjure drug in Louisiana. Many folks believe in the teaching of these alleged savants.
They believe that the Sprinkling of certain kinds
of oil around their home or annointing their body
with the oil would bring Luck or drive away evil.
We sell this highly perfumed oil but make no
claims that it will Brink Luck or Drive Away Evil,
or that it has any value for so-called conjure

FIGURE 1

TABLE 6

LIST OF ITEMS SOLD BY PRACTITIONERS AND IN DRUG STORES FOR USE
WITH MAGICO-RELIGIOUS PRACTICES

Incense and Incense Powders--Burned while reciting the psalms or special prayers.
Belief is that desires will be gained or prayers will be answered better. Also used in
spiritualist rites as sacrifice to the Deity and to drive away evil.
Candles (Plain and encased in glass devotional candles)--Used on altar by Spiritualist
ministers and practitioners. Also burned privately by individuals either singly or in
groups as with the "New Orleans Spell" in which four coins (usually nickels) are arranged in the form of a cross with a small candle at the head and foot. Color of
candles and their meaning:

(As observed in Chicago)   (As cited by McKay (1940:76) in New York City)
 Green: to break up love affairs   Green: for material gain
 Red: for victory or success   Red: to win and increase love
 Pink: for victory or success   Pink: to invoke celestial happiness
 Blue: to gain or hold love   Blue: for peace
 Yellow: to acquire money   Yellow: for true devotion
 Black: to invoke evil spirits   Black: to ward off evil
 White: for peace and to uncross   White: for communion with the departed
  one's self, drive away evil   Purple: for self-mastery, power and domination
                                             over others
                                            Orange: for lucky dreams

Floor-wash (powder)--Used in scrub water when washing floors, scrubbing woodwork and
doorsteps; care is to be taken so as not to miss dark places (corners, closets, under
furniture and behind doors). Belief is that it attracts people to the user's home,
brings romance, drives away evil, and keeps husband home.
Room Spray (liquid)--Can also be poured into scrub water. Used basically the same as
Floor-wash and carried the same belief.
Sprinkling Salts--Same as above. Also used under bed and in dresser drawers.
Perfume--Placed on handkerchief, behind the ears and on clothes. Beliefs: success in
love, arouse the opposite sex, hold loved ones in their power. Some types are re-
commended by practitioners and used to conjure up luck, win money and love. This type
usually has a loadstone or a root in the bottle.

Oils--Van Van oil is popular with Louisiana practitioners. Sprinkled around the
home and anointed on the body. Belief is that it brings luck and drives away evil

Table 6, cont'd

spirits. Holy oil is popular with the Spiritualists. Rubbed on sprinkled on the
clothes, belief is that it brings luck in various undertakings.
Loadstone and Roots--Carried on the person for good luck and success in love.

purposes. <u>Thousands of bottles are sold.</u> No. A202A
60¢ including tax.

There are many devoutly religious Negroes who see little
or no conflict between religion and the practices of the
conjurer or mystic (Powdermaker 1939:286), and many of the
practitioners claim divine authority and use passages in
the Bible to sanction their practices. Chapter thirty-three
of the Book of Exodus is most frequently cited for the use
of incense, and the ritual of burning candles and incense
often includes the reading or recital of certain Psalms
(4, 8, 10, and 26) and special prayers to the Deity.

The various Spiritualist churches are independent auto-
nomous units. They seem to have developed from the expansion
of groups headed by practitioners or as churches organized
by ordained ministers who have adopted certain techniques
of the practitioners and incorporated them into a kind of
Christian ritual. The number of Spiritualist adherents is
small in comparison to those of orthodox and holiness belief,
but they too have steadily increased with the growth of the
urban Negro population. In the Chicago area, for example,
there were seventeen Spiritualist churches in 1928, and fifty-
one in 1938, when they represented ten percent of the Negro
churches (Drake 1945:414). In Chicago in 1956, within
eleven blocks of one street, twenty Spiritualist churches
were noted, all of the store-front type (there are three
such churches in regular church buildings with congregations

of over a thousand each) and bearing such titles as St. Paul
Divine Healing Temple, Mt. Holiness Healing Temple, Redeem-
ing Helping Hand Spiritual Temple, and Divine United
Spiritual Temple. Also, as opposed to orthodox Negro churches,
several were headed by women: Reverend Marcella Rogers of
St. John Spiritual Temple, Sister Lula Brown of the St.
Paul Spiritual Temple, and Mother Magnolia Thomas of the
Universal Spiritual Temple.

Services in these churches closely approximate those of
the Holiness group; thus, the same Protestant hymns and the
contemporary style of Negro religious music are used. The
largest Spiritual church in Chicago is a leader in developments in the contemporary Negro style and has a full-time
staff of four musicians plus a choir of several hundred
voices, well known through its performances on television
and commercial recordings. Worship in the spirit of the
"old-time" religion, with overt emotional behavior, singing,
and shouting, is also found, and healing is stressed. Like
the Holiness group, the Spiritualist churches draw their
membership largely from former Baptists and Methodists.

The Spiritualists differ from the Holiness people and
the orthodox groups in a number of respects: (1) the use
of some paraphernalia of the Catholic church including altar,
candles in glass casing (devotional candles), statues of
Saints, Mary and Christ, and certain vestments and head
pieces; (2) sale of candles, healing cloths, incense,

flowers, and charms in connection with church ritual; (3)
giving special blessing during services upon the placement
of consecrated money upon the altar; and, (4) modifying
the requirements of sanctified living, which seems designed
to attract those who cannot live up to the strictness of
sanctification. Gambling, policy, card-playing, and the
like are not "preached down"; instead, appeals are made to
those who indulge in these practices to come to church,
whatever their faults, and find their welcome.

Patterns of Religious Musical Expression

As there is variation in the class structure (which implies certain sociological variables within the population)
and religious identification and practice (which implies
cultural variation in degree) there is also variation in the
musical system involved.

	Group One	Group Two	Group Three
Denomi- nation	Presbyterian Congregational Episcopal Methodist	Negro Baptist Negro Methodist (large well es- tablished churches)	Holiness and Spiritualist churches-- Also store- front Negro Baptist and Negro Metho- dist churches
Religious pattern	Euroamerican religious patterns	Euroamerican and "shouting" religious patterns	"Shouting" religious pattern
Musical tradition	Congregational singing--Euro- american music tradition--one choir	Less congrega- tional singing Choir and Gos- pel Chorus Mixed U.S. Ne-	Congregational singing when there is no choir--United States Negro

Group One	Group Two	Group Three
	gro and Euro-American music tradition	music tradition
Social class membership	Mainly upper class	Middle and lower classes	Mainly lower class

Of all variables considered, religious affiliation appears to be primary in determining commitment to a musical system. The variation of a musical style is found to range from a tradition almost completely in keeping with the musical system derived from a synthesis of European and African music values to an absolute commitment to the Euroamerican church song tradition.

The churches in Group One follow the Anglo-American church song tradition, whose concept of church music embodies the element of "sincerity, reverence, dignity, beauty, and simplicity" (McCutchan 1945:36), as viewed by Euroamerican standards. Music for congregational singing is sung from denominational hymnals created under the influence of English Calvinism (Watts and Wesley), nineteenth century American and English Evangelical hymns, and American Unitarian Hymns. These churches employ one choir which sings church-approved anthems in addition to songs from the hymnals. The gospel hymns of the 1870's, which developed out of the camp meetings of the early decades of the nineteenth century and were perpetuated under the influence of Moody and Sankey, are conspicuously absent in these churches.

Music in the churches of Group Two is coincident with
two musical traditions, the Anglo-American tradition, with
emphasis on the Moody-Sankey type, and the United States
Negro tradition in its contemporary manifestation. The
larger churches most often use two choirs in their services
in order to satisfy the musical tastes of their congregations
which are mixed in their commitment to a musical tradition.
The two choirs take the form of a Senior Choir, which sings
hymns and anthems from the Euroamerican tradition, and a
chorus which sings only songs in the United States Negro
tradition. Where only one choir is maintained, it sings in
both traditions.

Music employed in the churches of Group Three consists
of contemporary Negro religious songs, old hymns largely
from the Moody-Sankey collections, and songs from the
spiritual-jubilee tradition, with the latter two most frequently sung in the contemporary style. Music seems to be
a more important part of services in these churches than it
is among those of Groups One and Two, and musical performance
often consumes as much as fifty percent of the time allotted
to services. In keeping with the character of religious behavior, the music is highly emotional and rhythmic and
initiates or accelerates outbursts of emotion and forms of
possession among individuals. One choir is used for all
parts of the services, although smaller groups and soloists
sometimes supplement the musical offerings.

The music employed in these churches is referred to as "Gospel" music. The extent of commitment to the gospel idiom by members of these churches is evidenced, not only by the predominance of this type of music over other types employed in church services and its importance as a feature of such services in terms of the time allotted it, but also by the frequency with which it is found outside regular church services. In the Chicago area, for example, at least ten churches have special one-hour broadcast services on four different radio stations in which gospel music consumes approximately one-half of the time allotted. In addition to the numerous music dealers and four publishing houses, records and items of printed music are sold in some tailor shops, beauty shops, and in stores that feature religious paraphernalia. Religious disc-jockeys, who feature gospel, are programmed daily over several radio stations. Many churches, large and small, emphasize programs featuring gospel music exclusively, and independent promoters frequently use churches and public auditoriums to stage extravaganzas of gospel-singing groups.

Music of the Shouting Church

The gospel music tradition of culturally conservative Negroes in the middle and lower socio-economic strata is the major concern of this study. However, in establishing its relation to antecedent traditions one must keep in mind the

fact that there has been an overlapping, in time, of the
various styles of United States Negro religious music, and
that each style has been dominant in successive periods.
The spiritual-jubilee tradition and the jubilee singers
tradition are the earlier types known to have developed among
the African and African-derived population in the United
States, while the gospel tradition is the most recent musical development which dates from the beginning of the twentieth century, just prior to the time that Negroes began
to publish their own religious music.

The jubilee-spiritual tradition is still in evidence,
though largely confined to rural areas. As late as the
1920's, not only were the old songs of the tradition cited
as being sung, but new songs were being created by rural
southern Negroes.

> There is neither piano, nor organ....Presently,
> they will begin to sing, anyone who wishes starting
> a hymn. Little attention is given to the words, it
> is the melody that is important. Oh, how they sing!
> ...Strangely sweet and plaintive are the old folk
> songs--sorrow songs that were born long ago in the
> suffering hearts of black slaves. Soprano voices...
> contraltos...heavy basses add volume and round out
> the rhythmic cadence and harmony that can be heard
> only from our dark-skinned brothers of the South.
> Some of their songs will be new to a Northerner but
> sooner or later in the service those incomparable
> old songs "Swing Low Sweet Chariot" and "Roll, Jordan,
> Roll" are heard (Snyder 1920:169-71).

Or again:

> Not long ago Columbus, Mississippi, celebrated its
> one hundredth birthday. A unique feature of this
> Centennial celebration was the singing of plantation
> melodies by 75 negroes, taken from the cotton fields

in that section. They stood upon a bandstand that
had been erected on Main Street, dressed in plainest
garb, and sang for an hour to an interested audience
numbering thousands. Wild and original were the
songs they sang, not any of the well-known plantation melodies like 'Swing-Low, Sweet Chariot' or the
Foster compositions but chants perfectly original
both in words and tunes. They were the genuine negro
'spirituals' but none of them had ever been trans-
cribed or in any way reached the public. The singers
were country negroes who seldom visited town. Gen-
erations of them had been born and reared on Mississippi plantations and their folk-lore and songs came
down...from slavery times. They were absolutely inno-
cent of musical education...What they sang was not
frivolous or gay, but serious and melancholy, rather
monotonous, sounding like minor triads constantly repeated in various positions. The humor of the words
was often apparent to the audience and caused laugh-
ter, but the singers being wholly unconscious of
their blundering version of the scriptures sang on
seriously...so seriously and earnestly that one good
old sister got to shouting and fell in a trance,
causing another to exclaim in disgust, 'Dar now,
she done spile it all.' (Graham 1922:744).

In addition to the creation of new songs by relatively isolated
groups, individual composers in less isolated areas sometimes
claimed credit for compositions. Such composers travelled
from church to church singing their songs and teaching them
by rote to congregations, and those "ballets" which became
popular were printed on strips of paper (words only) and
sold to members of congregations for five cents each (Kennedy
1924:xxiii).

Jubilee singers, who were influenced by the Fisk tradition, were very popular as late as the 1940's, and those
groups composed of trained musicians, such as "The Charioteers,"
"The Deep River Boys," and "The Southernaires," enjoyed
national popularity through their recordings for major

recording companies, concert appearances, and radio performances. The Southernaires, who were trained at Hampton
Institute, appeared for many months on the stage of the
Capitol Theater in New York City in 1930, and enjoyed a long-
term coast-to-coast radio network program in addition to a
career on local New York City radio stations WMAC and WRNY.
The majority of these groups, however, were composed of untrained musicians who rarely recorded, and then only on
minor lables; thus, such groups as "The Dixiares," "The
Five Blind Boys," and the "Sunset Four" (Fig. 2) were known
only to devotees of the "old-time" religion. Most of the
groups of trained singers have now either disbanded or
entered the field of popular music, while the untrained
jubilee singers have been incorporated into the gospel tradition.

Although their style is considered as "old-time" or
"country," the fact that untrained jubilee singers are accepted by adherents of the new tradition in Negro religious
music indicates a relation between the two musical styles.
Like the small "gospel" groups, the untrained jubilee singers
usually perform in small groups of four or five persons, but
their performances are usually a cappella (sometimes accompanied by a guitar), while the gospel groups are always accompanied by either piano, or organ, sometimes both. The
call-and-response pattern of the spiritual tradition is also

FIGURE 2   ADVERTISEMENT C. 1926

characteristic of jubilee singers, but, in terms of harmony, the concept of specific vocal parts is more fully developed here than in the older spiritual tradition. The bass line is well developed and the lead singer often sings an obligato melody; however, the groups lack precision in that the middle voices often cross their parts, double the lead or bass lines, and cause parallel octaves and fifths in harmonic progressions.

The song type used by these groups differs from the standardized versions of trained groups and is quite similar to the song sermons or railroad songs of the earlier period (Barton 1898:713). This type of song consists of a refrain which alternates with a series of improvised verses sung by a leader. In the improvised portion the leader spontaneously creates verse and melody over a short repetitive rhythmic pattern set by the chorus. The harmony of the chorus phrase is of simple structure (one or two chords), and thus the melodic line of the leader, except for occasional wide skips, is narrow in range.

The gospel tradition was influenced by the older styles of Negro religious music, and here the split of Holiness groups from the orthodox Negro church was an important event, for it was among the Holiness groups that the free expression of religious and musical behavior common to the rural Southern Negro began to assert itself and undergo further development in an urban setting. Speaking of the influence of the music style of the Southern rural Negro one noted performer

(Mahalia Jackson 1958) stated:

> This kind of music was always in the Methodist
> and Baptist churches. The Baptists were first...
> would sing songs with a cry...then the Methodists.
> The Baptist had the largest denomination...
> they had soul singing and feeling and a high
> emotional service that expressed the spirituals
> more...because the Baptists gave vent to their
> feelings much easier than the Methodists, es-
> pecially the foot-washing Primitive Baptists.
> Holiness people split from the Baptists and
> Methodists...had more free expression of soul.

As with other aspects of religion, the Holiness people in-

tensified some of the aspects of the religious musical

tradition and introduced certain innovations.

> The Church of God in Christ started using drums,
> tambourines, triangles, and guitars. They
> started as "Triumph the Church of God That Never
> Dies", under Bishops Johnson and Mason. Mason
> did not believe in the idea that one never dies,
> and he split from the Triumph Church and founded
> the Church of God in Christ. There are others
> called "Jesus Only", "Fire Baptized", "Church of
> God and Saints" and so on. These were the first
> to have free will and express songs the way they
> felt within. If they felt to sing with a cry
> they did, and if they like singing with a "jubi-
> lee" feeling and dancing to the rhythm of the
> music they were expressing, they did so. That
> was the beginning of over-emphasizing certain
> things in religious music...like the rhythm.
> Today more people are bringing out the African
> rhythm in music (Jackson 1958).

While the use of instruments was forbidden in the orthodox

Negro church, their introduction by Holiness groups gave

the music a "different tempo and sound than just hand-

clapping" (Jackson 1958). Their version of Negro religious

music was regarded as something new, and the Church of God

in Christ (Holiness sect) is considered the primary influence
on the new gospel tradition which was emerging. The first
published Negro gospel songs (words and music) were those
of C. Albert Tindley.

> The name "gospels" was used around 1905-1906 when
> C. Albert Tindley was writing songs. I can
> remember...his "By and By"...this song was a
> great hit around 1907 in the churches of the
> South. They had no pianos but the sisters in the
> "Amen Corner" would carry the rhythm by patting
> their feet and clapping their hands (Dorsey 1956).

Tindley was a Methodist who wrote songs which were published
in Baptist Hymnals along with those of white composers, but
"...he was ahead of his time and his songs didn't go over
like Dorsey's which have been taken up by the big churches.
They didn't get on radio and records where they could become
popular" (Jackson 1958). The Holiness groups used Tindley's
songs as a model and began a repertory of religious folk
songs characterized by free expression and rhythmic instrumental accompaniment. But their emphasis on "soul-singing"
and use of the piano, guitar, and drums were regarded by
orthodox groups as a sinful attempt to replace the spirituals
with ragtime and blues tunes, and consequently, this musical
style tended to remain within their own groups.

The greatest personality in the gospel tradition is
Thomas A. Dorsey whose talents as a composer, publisher, performer, teacher, choir director and organizer have been more
influential on the tradition as a whole than those of any

other individual. Before shifting from secular to religious
music, in the late 1920's Dorsey enjoyed a wide reputation
among house-party crowds and theater audiences as jazz
pianist "Georgia Tom," and he accompanied and wrote songs
such as "The Stormy Sea Blues," for the famous blues singer
MaRainey, and "Tight Like That," for blues singing guitarist
Tampa Red. He played in bands with such well-known jazz
personalities as Les Hite and Lionel Hampton and arranged
music for Brunswick and Vocalion recording companies, but
after surviving a serious illness, Dorsey dedicated his
talents to the service of God and the Church.

> From about 1911 to 1916 I had little interest in
> spiritual things. I played piano in dance halls,
> theaters, and house-parties around Atlanta,
> Georgia. I wrote those kind of double-meaning
> songs that made big hits at stag parties. I never
> thought that God might care how I had used the
> talent he had given me. My main interest was in
> jump music and I gave little thought to playing
> hymns and gospel songs. Oh, I used to play at
> Sunday school occasionally just to please my
> parents, but I was more interested in the kind of
> music that you don't hear in the church. About
> that time I married Nettie Harper. She was a
> wonderful wife and an inspiration to me. But
> traveling together with a band, I felt that
> something was missing in our lives. Then one day
> I took sick and felt terrible but the doctor
> couldn't find anything wrong with me. I had to
> quit working but my faithful wife took care of
> me, spending her days working in a laundry and
> her nights nursing me. We were in Chicago then
> and this ordeal went on for a whole year. With
> all her loving care I grew worse and had to be
> confined to a hospital. After a short while
> there the doctors gave me up and sent me home
> a pitiful skeleton weighing scarcely 117 pounds.
> Shortly after I arrived home from the hospital
> Nettie's sister invited me to go to church. I

went with her, and it was the first time in
years that I had given a serious thought to God.
After the service the minister and I had a little
chat and during the conversation he made me know
that God had too much work in store for me to
let me die. Later, at home, I prayed and told
God that I was ready to do his work. My health
began to improve and that very week I began to
do God's work...I wrote a song...a spiritual
song. It was a gospel hymn..."Someday, Somewhere."
From that point on my health was restored and
after playing the new hymn for Nettie, we both
dedicated our lives to doing God's work...writing
gospel songs (Dorsey 1957a).

Dorsey's success was due not only to his ability to
capture the spirit of "soul-singing" and to compose in that
idiom, but also to the fact that he reproduced both words
and music for sale on single sheets which could be purchased
for fifteen cents per copy. The only religious music available, prior to this time, was published in book form, and
songs of the gospel tradition were circulated by their composers on small sheets of paper which contained only the
words; the melodies were learned by rote from persons who
knew them. As the pioneer in the independent publication
of these songs in sheet music form, Dorsey gained the same
legendary stature that W. C. Handy, the "Father of the Blues,"
enjoyed in the field of secular music. In the music publishing business for over thirty-five years, Dorsey was followed
during the 1930's by Mr. Kenneth Morris, Mrs. Lillian Bowles,
and Mr. Theodore Frye, all of whom operate music publishing
houses in Chicago.

However, Dorsey's contributions to contemporary Negro

religious music extended beyond publication and composition.
In his promotional efforts as a publisher he tirelessly presented his music to numerous church congregations.

> At the time very few Gospel singers not to mention
> Gospel choirs existed...Many are the times I walked
> from church to church seeking a chance to introduce
> my songs, my feet soaked from snow, sleet and rain.
> I thanked God for the days that I could bring home
> a dollar and a half to Nettie. But fortune smiled
> upon us and this gospel style of singing became more
> and more popular. It wasn't long until I had a cata-
> logue of songs that were popular from coast to coast.
> To promote them I frequently travelled with my own
> groups giving programs (Dorsey 1957).

In doing so, he trained and accompanied scores of artists
who performed for him during those lean years when he fought
for recognition over the opposition of orthodox ministers and
church musicians. Among those who very early came under the
Dorsey influence while performing with him are such well
known singers as Mahalia Jackson, Sally Martin, Clara Ward,
and Roberta Martin.

In its early beginnings in the 1920's, the gospel style
was outlawed by most churches of orthodox tradition, but it
gradually gained acceptance, first as solos in the home and
in churches, and later by endorsement by the National Baptist
Convention (Negro) in Chicago in 1930. Thus the music style
spawned by the Holiness groups began to infiltrate the
orthodox Negro church.

> When the Baptist convention met in Chicago in
> 1930, that was the first time gospel music was
> expressed officially in that body. Dorsey had
> written two songs 'How about You' and 'Did you

See My Savior?' These songs swept the convention
and it seems that there was a frantic expression all
over the place the whole week and then it swept the
Nation. The style started from Chicago with the
bounce...true, honest, sincere expression in gospel
music (Mahalia Jackson 1958).

The inclusion of gospel music in the worship services of
orthodox Negro churches resulted in conflict with the established hymn-tune and spiritual traditions, and gospel
songs were first sung by groups which were separate from
the established Senior Choir. Such groups were termed Gospel
Choruses and, thus, gospel music continued to be considered
a lower class form.

Again the energy and talent of Thomas A. Dorsey was
focused upon the cause of gospel music. Recognizing the
need for concentrated efforts in order to gain respect for
the new music, he created the National Convention of Gospel
Choirs and Choruses, Inc. As director of the gospel choir
at Pilgrim Baptist Church in Chicago in 1932, he organized
a national convention of gospel singers with a nucleus of
some two hundred persons. In his twenty-fifth address as
President of that body in August, 1957, Mr. Dorsey told of
the opposition which the group faced in the early days:

There were some who were dubious, or wavered in
opinion as to the success of the convention. A
minister said to me there that week, this thing
is starting off too big and with too much public
notice and support, it can't last long. Another
friend said to me, I don't think this kind of
organization can hold out because gospel singing
is new and the people as a whole who like the
better music are not for it in our churches...

The papers, magazines and many of the choir directors
ripped us up and down the back, but I had only one
answer for all the critics, and it was this: If God
be for us then who can be against us: If one can
chase a thousand and two can put ten thousand to flight,
then surely a few of God's consecrated singers can
perfect an organization for his service and glory...
Gospel songs, gospel singing and gospel singers have
come a long ways, they have made great progress in the
past twenty-five years...Take the radio twenty-five
years ago. You didn't hear many gospel songs and if
you did it was an old spiritual or hymn from the
Sunday school book. There were no songs by the contemporary writers and very few religious songs used
at all. But now, on the radio, television and in
swank concert halls, not only in this country but in
Europe and other continents have these gospel singers
and songs appeared and songs are used by many religious
groups there (Dorsey 1957b).

The success of gospel music can be measured by the success of Dorsey's songs. The most famous of his more than
450 songs, "Precious Lord Take My Hand," has been published
in twenty-six different languages and released on recordings
in most European countries and in Australia.

I have been blessed to have mailed some of my songs
throughout the world and given permission to more
than one hundred hymnals to print "Precious Lord"
in these books throughout the world, including a
Jewish Hymnal in Tel Aviv, Israel. I couldn't
imagine a Jewish book concern wanting to print,
and sing a song of the Protestant church or by a
Protestant writer, but a Jewish friend explained
it saying that as much as the song text did carry
the name Lord; so it was "Precious Lord Take My
Hand" (Dorsey 1957b).

In the United States his songs have been sung and recorded
by scores of white artists: Red Foley, Eddie Arnold, Tennessee
Ernie, Morton Downey, Elvis Presley, The Voices of Walter
Shuman, and Fred Waring.

There are many opinions as to what constitutes a gospel
song, the most common holding that it consists simply of the
introduction of jazz rhythms and blues singing into the
church. However, as has been pointed out by those intimately
acquainted with Negro folk music, the secular and religious
music of the United States Negro are facets of a particular
mode of musical expression and are composed of the same elements of rhythm, melody, and harmony. As we have seen in
our discussion of Negro religious music in the early period,
it was often impossible to distinguish some religious from
secular songs, even from the point of view of verse lines.
In the case of gospel music, the characteristic "soul-singing"
style has a great similarity to that found in blues singing,
but it is in no sense foreign to the Negro religious musical
style.

> What some people call the 'blues singing feeling'
> is expressed by the Church of God in Christ. Songs
> like 'The Lord Followed Me' became so emotional...
> almost lead to panic. But the blues was here be-
> fore they called it blues. This kind of song came
> after spirituals. The old folk prayed to God be-
> cause they were in an oppressed condition. While
> in slavery they got a different kind of blues.
> Take these later songs like 'Summertime' its the
> same as 'Sometimes I Feel Like a Motherless Child'
> (old spiritual), which had the blue note in it.
> The basic thing is soul feeling. The same in blues
> as in spirituals. And also with gospel music. It
> is soul music. When they talk about jazz, the
> Holiness people had it before it came in. They
> would take a song like 'What a Friend We Have in
> Jesus' and give it personal expression. They gave
> it a joyful expression...expressed things they
> couldn't speak. Some called it jazz because the
> beat is so strong. There's some gospel music on

the beat, after the beat and between the beat. They
called it gospel music for years but it did not come
into its own until way late...when the Holiness
people helped to emphasize the beat (Mahalia Jackson
1958).

The close relationship of jazz and religious music is
demonstrated by the ease with which contemporary performers
move from one area of music to the other. This is especially
noticeable among singers, and an imposing array of Negro
artists in the popular field received their basic musical
training in religious music and were performers in church
choirs or smaller singing groups prior to entering the jazz
field: Ray Charles, formerly of the Five Blind Boys; Nat
King Cole, who formerly sang and played with his father's
church in Chicago; Sarah Vaughn who started her singing
career in a Baptist choir in Newark, New Jersey; Dinah
Washington, a former gospel singer in Chicago; Billy Williams,
formerly with the Golden Gate Quartette; and Sam Cooke, formerly with the Soul Stirrers, are but a few. Further, a
large proportion of the Negro quartettes now performing in
"Rock and Roll" idiom began as gospel singing groups. At
the same time, there are many like Mahalia Jackson, who,
because of their deep religious convictions, refuse to enter
the jazz or blues fields.

Because its adherents recognize the close relationship
and similarity of gospel music to the older religious styles
(spirituals and jubiless), the more recent label "gospel"

tends to be applied to all types of Negro religious music.
Thus, "any song that talks about Christ is a gospel song, but
each age brings a new style. As soon as the composer talks
about Christ he is talking the 'Good News'...the Gospel.
However, spirituals and arrangements of white songs are not
true gospel songs" (Morris 1956). Gospel songs share two
major characteristics with the older forms of Negro religious
music. In the first place, they are emotionally inspired--
by visions, trouble, sorrow, thanksgiving, and joy. It is
quite common, during public performance, for a singer or composer to pause and tell the audience what inspired the composition he is about to sing. Thus, "one Sunday night...
this song came to me. It seems as though the melody floated
to my ear on whispered tones from beyond. I lost track of
what I was doing or even where I was and when I came to, I
found myself at the piano singing and playing this song."
(Bradford 1957). The second characteristic common to these
types of Negro religious music is variation and individual
interpretation in performance. Earlier unwritten forms were
subject to individual interpretation. The modern written
form is also interpreted individually, the music serving
mainly as a guide to the performer. A song is rarely, if
ever, sung "straight," and the same may be said of accompaniment, and an unusually high premium is placed upon individual
ability in improvisation.

Although used in more than one sense, the label "gospel"
is most appropriately applied to the contemporary religious
musical development in Negro churches which, while including
certain elements of the older styles, has a more "progressive"
character than its musical antecedents. This idea of progress is expressed in terms of the introduction of instrumental accompaniment and in the pattern of free melodic,
rhythmic, and harmonic interpretation. Thus, inventiveness
is a primary consideration of Negro gospel song composers
and performers.

Gospel music seems to have gained prominence because its
producers have been successful in absorbing and reflecting
the admiration of their public for innovation. Hence, the
musical reservoir of the group is constantly enriched by new
rhythms in old songs, invented and borrowed techniques of
improvisation, and the production of new songs. One of the
foremost composers uses a tape recorder with which he records
the singing of congregations, soloists, and vocal groups
in order to absorb music values and techniques for his own
compositions and arrangements. Thus, the gospel style, although appearing in written form, exceeds the limitations
of that form in that it is rarely sung exactly as written,
and at the same time affects the production of printed
compositions.

The publishers and composers, recognizing the desire for
improvisation and individual interpretation, as well as the

low level of academic musical training of their public, write
the music as simply as possible. Publisher and composer
Kenneth Morris summarizes their position:

> We don't write it too difficult by including all
> of the harmony. The people who play it are not
> interested in harmony. There is no attempt to
> include perfect cadences and the like. It's not
> written for trained musicians...(it is) written
> for second graders so to speak. A musician is a
> slave to notes. It's not written for that kind
> of person. It's written for a person who can get
> the melody and words and interpret the song for
> himself. We give only the basic idea and the
> person suits his own concept. If it were written
> correctly, we would go out of business. They
> wouldn't buy it...too complicated (Morris 1956).

As a consequence, different versions of Negro gospel songs are
published for white and Negro consumption. The versions for
white musical groups are scored in a musically correct and
complete fashion with various vocal parts--soprano, alto,
tenor and bass--in addition to the accompaniment; some are
even done in shape note style for performers in that idiom.
The versions produced for the Negro market, on the other hand,
often violate the rules of conventional harmony and include
only the bare essentials of a vocal line and piano accompaniment. The high percentage of white patronage (Dorsey, for
example, counts some 60% white trade) seems at first glance
out of proportion, until it is recognized that Negro singers
make less use of printed music than might be supposed. As
one publisher advises: "Negroes don't buy much music. A
white chorus of one hundred voices will buy one hundred

copies of a song. A Negro chorus of the same size will buy
two: One for the director and one for the pianist" (Dorsey
1956).

While small groups and solo singing are common features,
the gospel music currently sung for regular church services
is performed mainly by a choir. The form is primarily a
leader-chorus pattern in which the solo (leader) part is sung
by the director or solo voice from the choir. Some of the
larger churches have as many as ten "extra" singing groups
within the church, ranging in size from trios to small choirs
of about twenty persons, and these groups perform when the
regular choir is absent or on special occasions. A surpris-
ing number of store-front and other small churches maintain
choirs and electronic organs. Where this is not the case
the singing is congregational, led by the pastor or a member
of the congregation, and accompanied by a pianist if one is
available. If a choir is maintained, the congregation is
limited generally to the singing of the "Lord's Prayer" and
a hymn led by the pastor. Audience participation is usually
confined to hand-clapping, foot-tapping, and an occasional
"Amen" or other suitable interjection such as, "Go on up now."

A considerable number of choir directors are musically
untrained; many are unable to read music or to play musical
instruments. Recognition of this fact has inspired a well-
known leader in the field of gospel music to suggest that

directors and pianists "work together in close harmony and
agree on their interpretation of a new song before they re-
hearse the choir" (Windom 1951:14). Again, there are some
academically trained musicians, especially in the larger
churches, who hold degrees from accredited schools of music,
and arrange for and regularly direct groups of over one
hundred voices.

The greater proportion of choir members is also untrained;
many are quite "unmusical" in vocal quality and training and
the ability to read music. Thus during rehearsals, especially when learning new material, the various sections of the
choir are frequently dependent upon key individuals for correct pitch and time, and in some cases ability to read words
as well as music. The rehearsal of new material is a process
of rote learning, based on monotonous repetition in which
the pianist emphasizes individual parts--soprano, alto, tenor,
base--until the various sections have learned their parts
well enough for ensemble work. Even with intensive rehearsals,
the performances of songs are never identical and are characterized by the crossing of vocal parts, parallel fifths and
octaves, and individual embellishment of melodic lines. All
of this indicates that rehearsals merely serve to familiarize
choir members with the words and melody upon which they pro-
ceed to work out individual interpretations within their
vocal ranges. Depending upon the difficulties involved--music

learning problems, absenteeism, and membership (choir) approval
of a song--from two to six weeks may be spent in learning new
songs well enough for public performance.

Many choirs, especially those in small churches, lack
the personnel to fill some sections; these are usually the
male voices, particularly the tenors. Generally speaking,
women dominate the choirs, since small group singing appears
to be preferred by men; this seems to be related to the tradition
of jubilee singing groups among men and also to the fact that
women make up a larger percentage of the church-going population and are more active in the auxiliary functions of the
church, i.e., charity clubs, missionary societies, fund-raising
groups, and other service organizations. Further, the pres-
tige of professional status generally accorded to small groups
makes them more attractive to men, while the hardship of
traveling from place to place and other difficulties not encountered by choirs makes the small groups less attractive to
women. Thus, of more than forty small singing groups observed, seven were all female, four were mixed, and twenty-
nine were all male.

The gospel music sung by small groups appears to function largely in the area of entertainment; although falling
within the religious complex it is not a necessary part of
worship services. These groups perform on musical programs
presented both by church and by independent promoters. A
number of them are professional groups who are nationally

known and who travel across the country giving performances; they may also have contracts with recording companies. Some groups may be classified as semi-professional in that they do not earn their living by singing; often their performances are presented without charge, but with a view toward obtaining paid performances on programs under their sponsorship. The amateur groups are, for the most part, those who have not gained a large enough following to demand pay for their services.

In musical performance, the members of small groups usually exhibit greater musical talent than that observed in most choirs. Printed music is never used, but rehearsal techniques indicate that this is not important, for the arrangements appear to be worked out intuitively. A melody is stated by one of the upper voices and is harmonized by the lower voices in their natural ranges with the exception of the obbligato tenor who often sings a "falsetto" soprano. The ability to feel the individual part in relation to the harmony implied is of utmost importance. Since each part is carried by one person, musicianship, especially in intonation and blending, is of greater significance here than in choirs where poor musicianship can be hidden and go unnoticed. Arrangements appear to be the result of experimentation with the ideas of various group members as well as the imitation of the successful techniques of other groups. The latter fact is particularly true of the rhythmic patterns, ensemble phrasing, and vocal style in individual parts. Outstanding professional groups have distinctive styles which are often copied by lesser groups.

As with the various groups affiliated with church life, appearance is of importance and this is most frequently expressed in the use of uniforms or other symbols of membership. However, the universal use of robes and caps as a symbol of singing-group affiliation is less frequent among small groups than among choirs and choruses. The majority of small groups dress in street clothes, the male groups in suits of the same material, cut, and color. Frequently the main soloist dresses differently from other members of the group. Some of the younger male groups dress in sport jackets with contrasting trousers, and "process" their hair--a trait most usually encountered among singers and performers in the jazz field. Such behavior, however, is viewed with disdain by the more conscientious adherents to the gospel idiom and it is felt that such deportment is not in keeping with the purpose and meaning of the music; thus it is advised: "In view of the fact that Gospel music is accepted everywhere... singers should be consecrated and be careful of the lives they lead as well as the clothes they wear" (Robinson 1951:14).

A major objective of the National Convention of Gospel Choirs and Choruses, Inc., is the development of high standards in the performance of music and principles of behavior for performers. To reach these objectives, Thomas A. Dorsey founded the Gospel School of Music[1] as an adjunct to the national convention organization in 1942, and included such courses as: "Ministry of Music in the Church," "Planning and Leading Christian Worship," and "Personal Christian Living." As Dorsey advises:

> We must keep gospel singing on a high level...
> We cannot do, act, or look like some of the
> singers. What I mean is this, we cannot sing
> this gospel and when the program is over go out
> to the hotels, taverns, good time joints and mix
> with the people of the world. We cannot be
> gospel singers and go around with a filthy mouth
> cursing, swearing, using scurrilous words, of-
> fensive language, and using the mouth for every
> and anything but decent language, clean words
> and respectable conversation...We just cannot look
> like some of the others. How would a gospel singer
> look after giving a soul stirring program the night
> before; here she comes down the street the next
> day with peddle pushers on...(Dorsey 1957b).

[1]In 1948 a permanent home for the school was established in a former mansion on Lake Park Avenue in Chicago.
The school has dormitory facilities and attracts students
from within and outside the city. Through a fund set up
and administered by the convention some students are admitted to study under scholarship provisions.

V. ANALYSIS OF MUSICAL STYLE

1. Method of Analysis

The method employed in the following analysis is currently
used in the Laboratory of Comparative Musicology at Northwestern University; it is based upon the research initiated
by von Hornbostel (1905:85-97;30-62) and subsequently ela-
borated by Kolinski (1936:491-740), Waterman (1943; Herskovits,
M. J. and Waterman 1949), and Merriam (1951;1957b; Freeman
and Merriam 1956). Its aim is the description of a musical
style in clearly objective terms, and in order to achieve this
goal a quantitative approach using various measurements on
selected musical components has been adopted; however, more
subjective evaluations are not entirely ignored.

Some of the musical aspects considered in this type of
analysis are described briefly below; they have been more
elaborately delineated by Kolinski (1936) and Merriam (1951;
1956;1957b).

Tonal range is determined by the measurement, in semitones, of the span from the lowest to the highest notes used
in the melodic line of a song. When these two points are
separated by an octave or more, the tonal range is regarded
as wide; when separated by less than an octave, the range is
considered to be narrow. The octave is regarded as unison
when an identical melodic line is sung an octave apart by

two voices or groups of voices (such as solo-chorus).

The measurement of <u>melodic direction and contour is</u>
based primarily upon the difference in semitones between certain critical tonal positions: beginning (B) and ending (E)
tones, beginning (B) and highest (H) tones, beginning (B)
and lowest (L) tones, ending (E) and highest (H) tones, and
ending (E) and lowest (L) tones. While there are almost
limitless possibilities of variation in melodic direction,
Merriam (1951:99) cites the beginning-ending tone relationship as "the most direct means of getting at the problem"
of overall melodic direction. Three obvious possibilities
are noted: (1) when the beginning tone is higher than the
ending tone, the overall melodic direction is downward,
(2) when the beginning and ending tones are identical the
overall melodic movement is level, and (3) when the beginning tone is lower than the ending tone, the overall melodic
movement is upward.

Internal variation of these three basic types is an
accepted probability, and Merriam (1951:99) cites five possibilities "in order to indicate the complexity of charting
melodic movement in detail."

(1) B is <u>identical with</u> (=) E, but <u>lower than</u> (-) H, and
<u>higher than</u> (+) L.

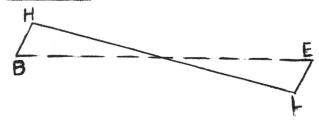

(2) B=H and E=L, but E and L ~ B and H.

(3) B=H, L~E and E~B.

(4) B=E, E=L.

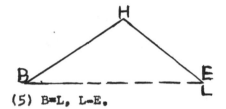

(5) B=L, L~E.

Melodic level is obtained by using the level formula
(the difference between the beginning tone as a percent of
the total tonal range and the ending tone as a percent of the
total tonal range) to derive the level difference. Thus, in
a song in which B=59° of the total tonal range and E=26° of
the total tonal range the level difference is -33°, express-
ing a downward melodic movement (Kolinski 1949:208,210).

Intervals and interval patterns are analyzed in quantitative fashion with the kind and number of all intervals used in songs noted. Further, the percentages of wide (five semitones or more), medium (four semitones) and narrow (three semitones or less), as well as the grouping of ascending and descending intervals are considered. The repetitive monotone (four or more successive tones sung on the same pitch) is also included in the analysis.

All patterns of intervals, including those encompassing thirds, fourths, fifths, and larger intervals are considered. These patterns are indicated by specific symbols (Kolinski 1936:491-740):

Triadic split fifth: the interval of a fifth broken into a melodic pattern of two successive thirds in which no intervening note may be present, i.e., C-E-G. The split fifth may be "dim" (diminished), "M" (major), "m" (minor), and either "f" (falling) or "r" (rising).

Linear thirds: three or more thirds moving successively in the same direction; falling (fff), i.e., B-G-E-C, or rising (rrr), i.e., C-E-G-B.

Interlocked thirds: the melodic pattern of up a third, down a second, and up a third (C-E-D-F), the overall direction either rising (r) or falling (f).

Pendular thirds: the repetitive pattern of a major or minor third, rising-falling-rising (rfr) or falling-rising-falling (frf), i.e., C-E-C-E (Mrfr). In patterns of fourths, two fourths rf or fr, linear fourths rr or ff, and interlocked fourths r or f are noted. Patterns of fifths and larger intervals as well as extended patterns are similarly considered.

Mode, duration tone and subjective tonic: Kolinski's system of analysis is used as the basis for the determination of modal structure (Kolinski 1936:491-740) and is explained as resting upon the functional relationship of the tones used, rather than solely upon the presence of a certain number of tones. The tonal center of the song (determined by actual duration), and the other tones used are placed upon the harmonic scale of seven consecutive fifths, from F to B; the mode is then determined by the number of these fifths which are encompassed by the tones of the song. For the sake of convenience (when the tones of a song encompass less than seven fifths of the harmonic scale) the mode is always transposed to "C," and similar transposition is used to eliminate accidentals. Songs in which the tones used encompass five fifths of the harmonic scale are designated a penta type, those which span six fifths, hexa, and those which span seven fifths, hepta. Tetratonic modes are found less frequently and less complex types (bi and tri) are relatively rare.

In analyzing modal structure the duration tone is determined by recording the number of times a tone is used, its duration and its position (do, re, mi, fa, sol, la, or si) in the scale upon which the mode is based. Thus, in the

modal structure CDAGE, if C is the duration tone, the mode
is typed penta do, if G, penta sol, and so on. In those instances in which two tones are of equal importance or duration,
both must be considered in determining the mode; thus, double
modal structures, i.e., penta do sol, hexa fa mi, appear.
It must be noted that the penta, hexa, and hepta modes may
utilize as few as two or three tones. Thus, a penta mode
may use the tones CGE and with C as its tonal center, may
be designated as 3:5:1, the first number representing the
number of tones used, the second number, the section of the
harmonic scale spanned, and the third, the third, the duration
tone.

While the duration tone is determined by quantitative
means, the subjective tonic refers to the subjective criterion of "key feeling" or tonality as this is observed in
the Western music tradition; and the two are included in
the analysis to determine the relationship between the duration tone and tonality in a particular style of music.

Explanation of the signs used in the transcriptions
and modal analysis may be given here. A over a tone indicates that it has been sharped less than a half-tone; while
a indicates that it has been flatted less than a half-
tone. A in the staff indicates a note that has no definite
pitch. A rising attack is indicated by a slanting line to
the right of a tone while a slanting line to the left
indicates a falling release; when between two tones or

a glissando is indicated. A   above a tone indicates accent.

In the modes the final tone is indicated by the
fermata   , while the reversed fermata   over a tone
indicates the beginning tone. The whole note   indicates
the duration tone, and the asterisk   designates the subjective tonic. Important intervals used in the songs are
indicated by the sign   , while the arrows used in this
sign   show the direction in which these intervals move.

The legend of each song in the transcriptions is based
upon the system used by Merriam (Merriam, Whinery and Fred
1956:173) in which pertinent information is abbreviated. For
example, in the heading Song S1:2u:108 the first figure (S1)
indicates that the song is number one in the collection of
spirituals; the designation G1 would indicate song one in
the collection of gospels; J1, song one in the collection
of jubilees; and A1, song one in the collection of instrument
accompaniments. The second figure (2u) indicates that the
original pitch was two semitones higher; the figure 2d would
indicate that the original pitch was two semitones lower.
The third figure (108) indicates that the tempo is 108 beats
per minute based upon the quarter note.

2. Analysis of Spirituals

Tonal range

The tonal ranges of spirituals include spans of eight
to sixteen semitones. Songs S1, S5, S9, and S10 have an
octave range (12 semitones) and Songs S2, S4, S7, and S8

use a range of 14 semitones. One song (S3) has a range of
sixteen semitones and one (S6) a range of eight semitones.
In general, then, the range of the spirituals is large, center-
ing about the interval of slightly more than an octave.

Melodic level, direction and contour

As expressed by the level formula 60°: 31°, the level
difference of this group of songs is -29°, and thus, the
general melodic direction is downward.

In terms of the beginning-ending tone relationship, the
beginning tone is more frequently above the final tone in a
range of from four to twelve semitones. In four songs (S2,
S4, S6, S7) the ending tone is four semitones below the initial tone, in two songs (S3 and S5) it is even semitones
below the initial tone, and in three songs (S1, S9, and S10)
the final and initial tones are the same.

The highest tone ranges from zero to twelve semitones
above the initial tone. In only one case is the initial tone
equal to the highest tone; in all other cases it falls below
it.

The range between the beginning tone and the lowest tone
is from zero to twelve semitones. In only one case (S9) does
the beginning tone equal the lowest tone. In songs (S2, S4,
S6, and S7) the initial tone is nine semitones above the
lowest tone, in songs S3 and S8 it is twelve semitones above
and in songs S1 and S5, it is five and seven semitones above
respectively.

A more consistent distribution characterizes the range
between the ending tone and the lowest tone; the latter
ranges from zero to seven semitones below the former. In six
songs, the ending tone is five semitones above the lowest
tone, in three songs the lowest and final tones are equal,
and in one song the ending tone is seven semitones above the
lowest tone.

The range between the ending and the highest tone spans
from eight to sixteen semitones; in all songs the highest
tone is found above the ending tone. In songs S1, S5, and
S10 the distance between the two points is twelve semitones;
in songs S2, S4, and S7 and S8 the range is fourteen semitones,
and in S6 the distance is eight semitones.

The relationships between the kinds of tones considered
here indicate both upward and downward melodic movement.
Upward internal melodic movement is indicated by the fact
that the distance between the intitial and final tones never
equals the total tonal range of a song, and further, the
initial tone (except in one case, S6) is consistently below
the highest tone. Downward internal melodic movement is indicated by the fact that the initial tone (except in one
case, S9) is consistently above the lowest tone. This variation in relationship is expressed in five general outline
type of melodic contour (Fig. 3).

Melodic intervals

Of 1007 ascending intervals, the major second is most

Fig. 3 DIAGRAM OF MELODIC CONTOUR IN SPIRITUALS

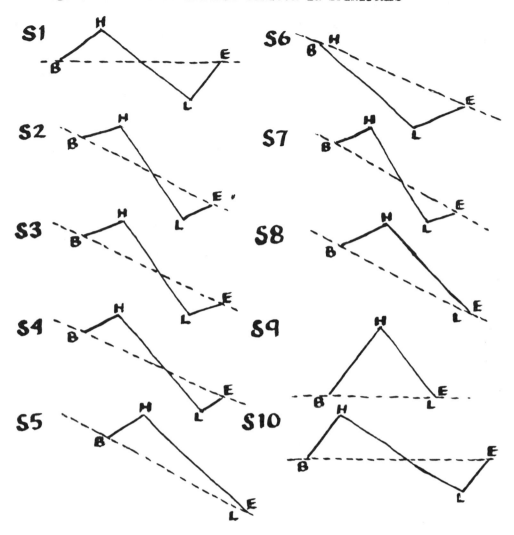

frequently used, 32.4%, followed respectively by the major
third, 24.6%, minor third, 20.1%, minor second, 9.6%, perfect
fourth, 7.1%, and perfect fifth, 3%. The augmented fourth,

augmented fifth, major sixth, minor seventh, major seventh, and octave account for less than 3% of the total ascending intervals.

Of 1276 descending intervals the major second is most frequently used, 37.8%, followed by the major third, 23.7%, minor third, 20.6%, minor second 9.4%, perfect fourth, 6.1%, and augmented fourth, 1%. The perfect fifth, augmented fifth, and the octave together account for less than 1% of the total descending intervals used.

Of the total 2283 ascending and descending intervals, the major second is used most frequently, 35.4%, followed by the major third, 24%, minor third, 20.6%, minor second, 9.4%, perfect fourth, 6.9%, perfect fifth, 1.8%, and augmented fourth, 1%. The augmented fifth, major sixth, minor seventh, major seventh, and octave together account for less than 1% of the total intervals used.

Twelve kinds of intervals are used ascending and nine descending; the three kinds of intervals used ascending, but not descending are the major sixth, minor seventh, and major seventh.

Descending intervals make up 55.9% of the total intervals used, while ascending intervals represent 44.1% of the total. Sixty-five and two-tenths percent of the intervals used are narrow, that is a minor third or less, 24% are medium, that is, a major third, and 10.8% are wide, that is, greater than a major third.

In summary, melodic interval usage in this group of spirituals is characterized by a high percentage of narrow intervals and a relatively low percentage of wide intervals. Descending intervals are used approximately ten percent more than ascending intervals; this correlates, of course, with the descending melodic direction. While there is a high percentage of major seconds, major thirds and minor thirds are also of special importance; the minor second and perfect fourth constitute noticeable percentages, while larger intervals are of much less consequence.

Melodic interval patterns

The triadic split fifth is found in eight songs (S1, S2, S3, S4, S6, S7, S8, and S9). Of the forty-two such melodic interval patterns used, four are dim f, twenty-one Mr, seven Mf, seven mr, and three mf. Song S9 is strongly influenced by this pattern and includes seventeen split fifths, ten of which are mr, seven dim f and three Mf; no split fifth patterns are found in Songs S5 and S10.

Pendular thirds are used in six songs, S1, S3, S4, S5, S6, and S9. Of the forty-one such patterns used, three are Mrfr, twenty-two Mfrf, and two Mrfr; in addition, seven Mrfrf and six Mfrfrf are of an extended type. The pattern of pendular thirds appears to be of structural importance in four of these songs (S3, S4, and S6); song S3, for example, contains eighteen pendular thirds of which eight are Mrfr, one Mfrf, one mfrf, six Mfrfrf, and two Mrfrf. Interlocked thirds are found but once in this group of songs (S2).

Interval patterns of two fourths are found in five songs, and five of eleven such patterns appear in song S5. No interval patterns larger than a perfect fourth are to be found. The interval of a third (major and minor) appears to be of special importance in these songs since it dominates the interval patterns.

The repetitive monotone is present in all of the songs; patterns of 4, 5, and 9 are used in Song S10 and at the other extreme, a single repetitive pattern of four notes is used in Song S9. The repetitive monotone is found at the beginning, ending and in the middle of phrases, and is clearly a characteristic of this group of songs.

Ornamentation and melodic devices

The use of ornamental devices (rising attack, glissando, falling release, and melodic accents) is characteristic of this group of songs. In addition, vocal embellishment (from two to five notes per syllable) is quite common and appears in the following patterns: (1) scalewise major seconds (Fig. 4), (2) scalewise major seconds followed by the skip of a third (Fig. 5), (3) scalewise major seconds followed by a pattern of thirds (Fig. 6), (4) interlocked thirds (Fig. 7), (5) pendular major seconds (Fig. 11), and (6) triadic split fifths (Fig. 9).

While the musical style under consideration is essentially melodic, the use of non-harmonic tones may be noted; such

accessory tones are identified in the Western musical system
as appogiatura (AP) and auxiliary tones (X), as for example
in Figs. 4, 5, 6, and 8.

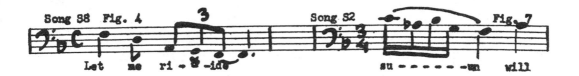

Syncopation and its extension are achieved by the
offbeat phrasing of melodic accents in which the latter
consistently fall on the weak part of the beat (Fig. 10)
sometimes anticipating the strong beat over the bar line
(Fig. 11).

Song S9   Fig. 10

Oh — —   Oh —   death   is   aw - - - ful   Ah - - -   death

Song S3   Fig. 11

I   went down   the hill   the   o-ther day   some - bo-dy   well sing

Melodic meter and durational values

Leader and chorus lines are sung in the same meter in all songs: eight songs are in 4/4, one in 2/4, and one in 3/4.

Fourteen kinds of durational values are used, among them the eighth note, 43.2%, the quarter note, 25.6%, sixteenth note, 9.2%, dotted eighth note, 3.6%, eighth note tied to a half note (frequently over the bar line), 2.1%, and the dotted half note, 1.4%. The sixteenth note tied to a quarter note, triplet values of eighth notes, whole note, dotted sixteenth note and thirty-second note together account for less than three percent of the total kinds of durational values used. A wide variety of durational values seems to be characteristic of this group of spirituals.

Formal structure

A general characteristic of the formal structure of all the songs is the overlapping call-and-response pattern in which the leader's phrase alternates with the chorus phrase. Within this overall formal structure, three types are

observable: (1) short-phrase leader and chorus pattern, as
in Song S8; (2) long-phrase leader and chorus pattern, as
in Song S9; and (3) short-phrase leader and chorus pattern
followed by a long chorus phrase, as in Songs S4, S3, and S10.
The overlapping of leader and chorus phrases is not extensive
in these songs.

In the performance of four other songs (S1, S5, S6, and
S7) the overlapping of leader and chorus is more extensive;
this occurs primarily in congregational singing where the
simultaneous individual interpretation of a melodic line
produces a polyphonic effect. In such cases the leader indicates the order of verses by introducing the first or key
word, and this pattern is clearly marked in the performance
of Songs S1, S5, S6, and S7. Examples from Song S1 (Fig. 12)
and Song S5 (Fig. 13) illustrate the point.

Although the singing of spirituals is traditionally a
group performance in which the overlapping leader-chorus

Song S5   Fig. 13

(leader) look how they done my Lord   done my Lor - ord   done my Lo

(chorus)   Oh   done my Lord - -   done my Lord

pattern is a marked characteristic, the continuity and co-
hesiveness between the two parts is such that some of the
songs can be sung solo, as in the case of Song S2, without
destroying the effect of the usual leader and chorus phrases.

While the spirituals are characterized by an A phrase
sung by the leader and a B phrase sung by the chorus, they
show variation in the organization and internal structure
of phrase patterns. For example, several structures are
found in the leader lines; the repetitive patterns of a one-
unit melodic phrase, A(a) A(a) A(a'), as in Song S10; the
repetitive pattern of a two-part unit A(ab) A(ab), as in
Song S9; and the simple variation of single unit melodic
phrases A(a) A(b) A(b') A(c) A(b) A(d) A(d) A(e) A(d')
A(f), as in Song S4.

The phrase pattern of the chorus lines shows an equal
amount of variation in organization but tends to be more
complicated in internal structure. For example, Song S3

uses single, three-part, and four-part units; B(abc) B(c)
B(b'ab'c) B(b'ab'c), and in addition there are found repeti-
tion of a four-unit melodic phrase, B(a a' a b'), as in
Song S9; simple alternation of one-unit melodic phrases,
B(a) B(b) B(c) B(a), as in Song S8; and repetition of a one-
unit melodic phrase followed by a three-unit phrase, B(a)
B(a') B(a'') A(a''b c), as in Song S10.

In summary then, while the A-B (leader-chorus) pattern
of phrases is characteristic of the spirituals, there is a
considerable amount of variation in the patterning of phrases,
and multi-unit phrases are used. Within the overall formal
structure of leader (A) and chorus (B) patterning, three
types are identifiable; short-phrase, long-phrase, and a combination of short-phrase A-B and long-phrase chorus refrain.
Finally, overlapping is present in all songs; while it is
traditionally of short duration, in some of the songs it
is quite extensive and creates a polyphonic pattern.

Scale, mode, duration tone and subjective tonic

Four of the spirituals use some type of hepta mode,
three are pentatonic, and two are hexatonic. Of the hepta
structures, two are hepta do, but with fewer than seven tones,
forming the structures 5:7:1 (Song S3) and 4:7:1 (Song S9),
one is a normal hepta do structure 7:7:1, and the remaining
structure a normal hepta sol 7:7:5. The hexa structures are
hexa do, one a normal 6:6:1 and the other using fewer than

six tones to form a 5:6:1. The penta structures are penta do
with two a normal 5:5:1 and one a 4:5:1 utilizing less than
five tones. Thus, this group of songs is heterogeneous in
terms of mode. A hypothetical scale employing all the tones
used in the songs creates a chromatic scale encompassing an
octave and a perfect fifth. In terms of the number of tones
actually utilized (excluding octaves) two songs are hexatonic,
three are hepta, four octo, and one nona.

Special notice may be given to Song S4 in which there
is a shifting major-minor tonality by the leader, while the
chorus line implies a steady minor tonality in the first part
of the song; a clearly major tonality is established and
maintained throughout the second section both by leader and
chorus. In view of this, the song is not susceptible to modal
analysis; in all other songs a clearly major tonality is maintained and modal analysis is possible.

The duration tone and subjective tonic fall on the same
pitch in nine of the ten songs; in the one remaining song
the duration tone falls on the fifth degree of the scale.
Thus the relationship between the duration tone and the subjective tonic is direct in the majority of songs. There are
no modulations and in all songs the pitch remains fairly
constant, rising only a semitone from beginning to end, and
hence a strongly established tonality is maintained.

Tempo

Melodic tempi in the songs, based upon the quarter note,

range from 80 to 132 beats per minute, the slower tempi occurring in 2/4 (76-92) and 3/4 (76-80). The faster tempi
are in 4/4 and range from 108 to 132; six of these eight
songs cluster about the range of 108 to 112 beats per minute.
The amount of acceleration ranges from no appreciable increase
in tempo in Songs S1, S2, S3, S5, and S6, to as much as sixteen beats per minute in Song S4.

Summary

The spirituals under consideration were sung in the
traditional unaccompanied style of the early period in United
States Negro religious music. The tonal range centers around
the octave and is fairly homogeneous. The melodic level
formula 60° : 31° expresses a level difference of -29°, and
the general melodic contour is downward; upward and downward
internal melodic movement is clearly characteristic. The
songs are fairly homogeneous in interval usage, and although
a wide variety of intervals is used, there is a characteristic high percentage of major seconds and major and minor
thirds. Descending intervals are used more frequently than
ascending intervals. Patterns of thirds appear to be of
special importance; the repetitive monotone, found in all of
the songs, is also an outstanding characteristic. Ornamental
devices, including the rising attack, falling release, and
glissando are found, and special melodic configurations are
used. Syncopation and its extension are highly characteristic,

and the songs form a rather homogeneous grouping in terms
of melodic meter; a wide range of durational values is
employed.

The overlapping call-and-response pattern is of great
importance to all the songs, serving to create the overall
formal structure; the overlapping of leader and chorus
lines is extensive in some songs and results in polyphony.
A hypothetical scale based upon all notes used is chromatic, but the scales of the individual songs are hexa-,
octo-, and nonatonic. The modes used are of penta,
hexa, and hepta types. Although a shifting major-minor
tonality was present in part of one song and the
slight upward shift of a semi-tone in pitch was
present in all songs, a strong tonality is always present. Melodic tempi range from 80 to 132 beats per
minute based upon the quarter note, and acceleration in
most songs is slight.

In final summary, the spirituals contain characteristics which allow them to be classed as a homogeneous grouping
of songs, including similarity in tonal range, overall melodic
contour, general interval usage and use of certain interval
patterns, ornamental devices, overall formal structure,
melodic meter, durational values, and a cappella style. They
are heterogeneous, however, in terms of scale, mode, and
organization of phrase patterns.

Song S1;

won't be trou - ble more

won't be won- drin' an- more I won- der

where my mo - ther - er won - der where she

where my mo - ther I won - der where she

gon - on - one sit - tin' in

gon - on - one she's some where sit - tin' in th

King - dom won't be trou—ble no more

King— dom and she won't be trou - ble no more I'm

Lord I'm grie - vin' grie—vin'

grie—vin' Lord I'm grie—vin' I'm grie—in'

a - bout my so — — — o — — oul

a - bout my so — — 0 — — oul um no

Song S1

soo – – ner than   feet strike   Zi – – – – on   un

soon   than   my   feet strike   Zi – – – – on   I

won't   be   grie – – vin'   an – – y   more

won't   be   grie – vin'   an – – y   more

Song S2:76-80

Oh   the   su--un--un   will ne-ver   go

down --- go down oh the su------un will

ne--ver go dow------ow-ow go down   a   flow-er

a   bloo-ing   for   e--ver--er   more

then the su------un will ne-ver--- go down

don't   you   fee-ee--eel   like   shou--ting   some

time   some   time don't   you   fee-ee--eel   like

shout--ing   some   time   some   time   a

flow-er   a   bloom-ing   for   e--ver--er

more   then   the   sun   will   ne-ver   go

down don't you mi-i--iss   your   mo-ther

some time   some   time don't you miss

your mo- -the r --er   some   ti - - - - ime   some

time   a   flow - - er   a   bloo - - ming   for

e - - -ver - - - er   more   then   the   su - - - - - - - - - - un

will   ne - ver - - -   go   down.

Song S3:ld:112

Song S3

Song S3

go   my   Lord   ev' - ry   where I   go - - - - - -

some - bo -dy   talk - - -ing 'bout   Je - - sus.

Song S4: ld: 76—88

Song S4

183.

Song S5:3d:120

Song S5

mum - ble - - ing   word   not a   word   not   a   word

mumb - - -ling word   not a word   not a   word

did He   say Well they plan - ted Him a   thor - ny

did He   say - - -   thorn - Y

crown thor * ny crow- -own thor - ny crown They plan -ted

crown thor - ny crow - own thorn* ny crown

Him a   thor - ny   crow- -own He ne - ver said a   mum - ble

Him a   thor - ny   crow - - own   said a   mum - -

- -ing word   not a   word   not a   word   did He

- -blin' word   a   word   not a   word   did He

say   Well they placed it on His head   on His

say   Um - - - - - - - head   on His

Song S5

186 .

Song S6:2u:108

Song S6

Song S6

Song S7:104-108

(chorus)

(leader)

Ah ----- the blood   Ah ----- the blood ---- the

blood done signed my -- name ----   Ah the

blood done signed my   name--- Ah the blood

blood   Ah the blood   done sign my

Ah the blood   Ah the blood done sign my

name   the blood   Ah --- blood

name   Ah --- the blood ---   Ah the blood

Ah --- the blood done sign my name Ah -- the

Ah -- the blood done sign my name Ah --- the

blood--- sign   my   name

blood   done sign ---ign my   name   how you

Song S7

Song S7

done sign my name in my heart - - - - in my

done sign my in my heart in my

heart - - - - Oh the blood done sign my name in my

heart Ah the blood done sign my name in my

Oh - - - - in my heart Oh - - - the blood done sign

heart - - in my heart Oh the blood done sign

my name Oh the blood done sign - - - my

my name Oh the blood - - done sign my

name.

name.

Song 88:5u:132

Song S8

Song S9

Song S10

3. Analysis of the Jubilee Style

Tonal range

In tonal range the songs are quite homogeneous in that
all use a range greater than the octave. The narrowest tonal
range is fourteen semitones--Song J7; the widest is twenty-six
semitones--Song J8. Since all of the songs have a range exceeding the octave, the group may be characterized as using
a wide tonal range.

Melodic level, direction, and contour

The melodic level of the jubilees is 30° : 29°; thus
the level difference is -1°. Melodic direction, as characterized by the beginning-ending tone relationship shows a
tendency toward an overall level melodic movement; the initial tone is most frequently identical with the final tone.
In six songs (J, J2, J3, J4, J7, and J10) the two tones are
equal, in two songs (J8 and J5) the initial tone is respectively five and twelve semitones below the final tone, and
in two songs (J6 and J9) the initial tone is seven semitones
above the final.

The highest tone is consistently above the beginning
tone, ranging from four semitones above in Song J9 to as
much as twenty-two semitones above in Song J1. The beginning-
lowest tone relationship is slightly less consistent and in
two songs (J1 and J7) the initial, lowest, and ending tones
are identical, while in all other songs the lowest tone
ranges from five to twelve semitones below the initial tone.

In two songs (J1 and J7) the ending and lowest tones are identical, while in all other cases the lowest tone is from five to seventeen semitones below the ending tone. The highest tone is consistently above the ending tone, ranging from four semitones above, as in Song J5 to as much as twenty-two semitones above, as in Song J1.

Upward internal melodic movement is strongly marked in these songs, and this is clearly seen in the fact that in all cases the highest note is above both the initial and final tones. Downward internal melodic movement is characteristic but less strongly marked; in all but two songs the lowest note is below both the initial and final tones.

Variation in the relationship between the kinds of tones considered here creates four types of melodic contour within this body of song (Fig. 14).

Melodic intervals

Of 790 ascending intervals, the major second is most frequently used (25.5%), followed closely by the minor third (24.8%), and the major third (22.9%). These intervals are followed in frequency of appearance by the minor second (14.8%), and the perfect fourth (10.3%), while the augmented fourth, perfect fifth, augmented fifth, major sixth, minor seventh, major seventh, octave, and two compound intervals account for less than two percent of the total ascending intervals. Each of the compound intervals appears but onee--

Fig. 14   DIAGRAM OF MELODIC CONTOUR IN JUBILEES

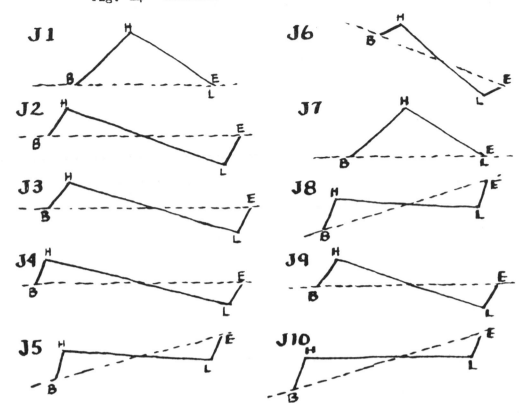

an octave and a perfect fourth (g to C'') in Song J7, and an octave and a minor third (D' to F'') in Song J3.

Of 1007 descending intervals, the major second is again the most frequently used (29.6%), followed by the minor third (23.3%), major third (18.4%), perfect fourth (7%), perfect fifth (4%), and the octave (1.4%). The augmented fourth, augmented fifth, major sixth, minor seventh, and major seventh account for less than two percent of the total descending intervals.

Of the total of 1797 ascending and descending intervals, the major second is used most frequently (27.9%), followed by the minor third (23.9%), major third (20.4%), minor second (14.2%), perfect fourth (8%), perfect fifth (3%), major sixth (1%), and the octave (1%). The augmented fourth, augmented fifth, minor seventh, major seventh, tenth, and eleventh account for but two percent of all intervals used.

Twelve kinds of intervals are used ascending and twelve descending. The major seventh and the eleventh are used ascending but not descending. Descending intervals account for 55.5% of the total intervals used, while ascending intervals represent 44.5%. Sixty-four and five-tenths percent of the intervals used are narrow, 19.4% are medium, and 16.1% are wide.

In terms of melodic interval usage, the jubilees employ a high percentage of narrow intervals. Major seconds are most frequently used and, while minor and major thirds are of slightly less importance individually, as a group thirds (major and minor) dominate this body of music.

Melodic interval patterns

The interval of a third (major and minor) appears to be of particular importance in the jubilees. Thus, the triadic split fifth is found in eight of the songs (J1, J2, J3, J4, J5, J6, J9, and J10). Of the thirty-two such melodic interval patterns used, one is dim r, one dim f, twenty Mr, three Mf,

four mr and three mf. Pendular thirds are found in all of
the songs including five Mfrf, three Mrfr, five mrfr, two
mfrf, one Mrfrf, one Mfrfr, and one mfrfr. No patterns of
interlocking thirds were observed.

Patterns of fourths appear eleven times and are found
in five songs (J5, J7, J8, J9, and J10). Ten of these are
patterns of two fourths of which eight are fr and two rf;
one pattern of pendular fourths frfr is found in Song S9.
Of the larger interval patterns used, two are patterns of
two fifths rf (Songs J4 and J5); a pattern of two sixths fr
(Song J10), and patterns of two octaves rf, are found once
in Song J8 and again in Song J4. Special attention may be
called to the compound interval pattern of down an octave
and up a major third which is of structural importance in
the leader's lines of Song S5.

The repetitive monotone is present in all the songs in
series of 4, 5, 6, 7, 8, 10, 11, and 14 notes. This pattern
appears to be of structural importance in the leader's improvised phrases where the melodic contour is generally level
but contains intermittent wide skips, as in Song J2 for
example (Fig. 15).

Ornamentation and melodic devices

The glissando, falling release, rising attack, and
melodic accents are found with great frequency in the jubilees.
In eight songs two notes per syllable frequently occur, and

Songs J1 and J7 are dominated by extremes in vocal embellishment. Melismatic devices in the latter songs range from
simple pendular and scale-wise ornamentations (Fig. 16) to
more complicated structures (Figs. 17 and 18).

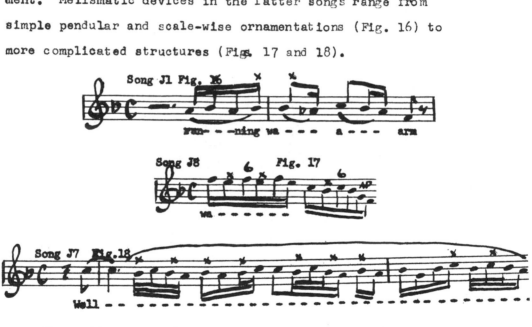

The patterns of alternation of principal tones, with
supplementary tones found within these melismatic structures,
may be described in Western musical terms as auxiliary tones
(X) and appoggiatura (AP).

Syncopation and its extension, offbeat phrasing of melodic accents, is a clear characteristic of these songs, and in company with the harmonic rhythm, forms part of an overall rhythmic pattern which will be dealt with below.

Melodic meter and durational values

The leader and chorus lines are sung in the same meter in all songs; eight songs are in 4/4 and two are in 2/4. Of the fourteen kinds of durational values used, the eighth note appears most frequently (52.3%), followed by the sixteenth note (16.3%), quarter note (15.1%), dotted quarter note (4.2%), dotted eighth note (3.5%), half note (3.2%), and thirty-second note (2.4%). The dotted sixteenth note tied to a quarter note is also found. A wide variety of durational value is thus characteristic of the jubilees.

Formal structure

The overall formal structure of the songs emphasizes overapping leader and chorus phrases. An additional principle of construction is employed in which identical sections (relatively fixed melody and verse) alternate with contrasting sections in which the leader improvises melody and verse above a repetitive chorus phrase. The two principles of construction are found in nine of the ten songs (Fig. 19).

The organization of phrase patterns in the identifying sections shows three general structures: (1) the repetitive pattern of a single phrase A(a a'), as in Song J4; (2) the

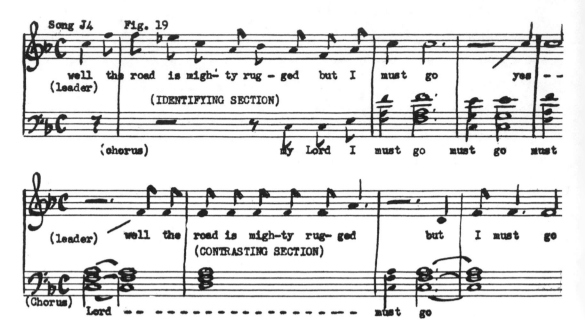

Song J4   Fig. 19

(leader)
well the road is migh-ty rug-ged but I must go   yes

(IDENTIFYING SECTION)

(chorus)
my Lord I must go must go must

(leader)
well the road is migh-ty rug-ged   but I must go

(CONTRASTING SECTION)

(Chorus)
Lord — — — — — — — — — — — must go

repeat of a multi-unit pattern (A(a b), as in Song J2, and
its extension A(abcd) as in Song J3, and (3) a rather complex
patterning of phrases A(abcdeff'fghi, and so on), as in
Song J10. With this organization of phrases there is further
complexity of leader-chorus patterning which employs several
devices: (1) leader introduces beginning of phrases (lead
frequently shifts from upper voice to the bass line) as in
Songs J10, J3, and J2; (2) long-phrase overlapping call-and-
response pattern, as in Songs J8 and J4; (3) long-phrase
leader lines over short repetitive chorus phrases, as in Song
J7; (4) a mixture of long-phrase and short-phrase leader lines

over short-phrase repetitive chorus response and long-phrase
call-and-response patterns, as in Song J6.

In the contrasting sections, the leader's lines show a
complex patterning of phrases which are improvised over
brisk repetitive rhythmic phrases sung by the chorus. The
chorus phrases are repetitive and less progressive than in
the identifying sections, and the improvised leader lines also
tend to be less progressive melodically, characteristically
including the repetitive monotone pattern (Fig. 19).

In summary, the formal structure of the jubilee is
based upon the leader and chorus, overlapping call-and-
response pattern, and the alternation of identifying sections
with contrasting sections dedicated to leader improvisation.

Harmony and harmonic rhythm

Interpretation of the harmonic vocabulary employed in
this musical style is based upon standards developed in the
Western music tradition during the eighteenth and nineteenth
centuries and is generally practiced in the religious music
of western culture at the present time.

The use of full harmony is a clear characteristic of
this style. The vocal parts are clearly conceived in terms
of the natural vocal ranges of the singers and the bass line
is well developed, often contributing lead phrases as in
Songs J2, J3, and J10; vocal ranges exceeding that of the
natural voice are sometimes employed, as in the use of

falsetto by the tenor lead in Song J1 (Figs. 20 and 21). The
performers are characteristically males who perform in units
of from four to six singers; sometimes a female lead voice
is employed, as in Songs J6 and J4.

All of the basic chords in the Western music system (I,
II, III, IV, V, VI, VII) are used and are found in root position, inverted, and four (seventh) and five factor (ninth)
chords. However, certain constructions and progressions which
are systematically avoided in Western music are found to be
characteristic of this style. The most characteristic harmonic
traits are (1) the use of parallel fifths and octaves (frequently caused by a distinctive practice of voice leading),
as for example, in Songs J0, J2, and J10 (Fig. 22), (2) the
use of irregular progressions and incomplete chords, as seen
in the cadence formulae of Songs J4, J5, J6, and J9 (Fig. 23),

and (3) the use of harmonic patterns as a rhythmic device
and indeed, in a manner which serves as a percussive resource.

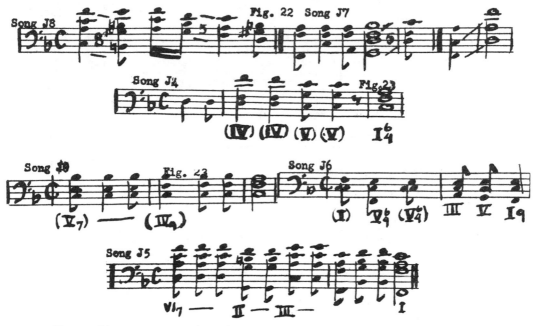

The following examples (Fig. 24) show how percussion-
type harmonic rhythm is used in this musical style to support
the offbeat phrasing in the leader's melodic line.

Fig. 24 cont'd

Scale, mode, duration tone, and subjective tonic

A hypothetical scale using all of the tones appearing
in these songs results in a chromatic scale which covers a
range of two octaves and a perfect fifth. In respect to the
number of tones used in each song, two are octo, three
nona, and five deca, not counting octaves. Modally, two
songs are pentatonic, two hexa, and four hepta. The penta
structures are of the normal 5:5:1 type. Of the hexa structures, one is hexa do 5:6:1, and one is a bi-modal hexa
do-sol structure, 5:6:1-5. The hepta structures also show
variation in that two are normal hepta do 7:7:1, and two
are hepta sol 6:7:1. Two songs (J2 and J8) were not susceptible to modal analysis due to their chromatic character.
The songs do not represent a homogeneous grouping in modality
(See appendix).

The jubilees show a strongly established tonality with
no cases of modulation. The duration tone and subjective

tonic fall on the same pitch in eight songs; in the two
remaining songs the duration tone falls on the fifth degree
of the subjective tonic scale.

Tempo

Melodic tempi in this group of songs, based upon the
quarter note, range from 60 to 153 beats per minute. The
tempi in seven of the ten songs range between 70 and 96
beats per minute; the tempo in one song (J7=60) is lower than
70 and the tempi of two songs are above 100 beats per minute
(J2=152, J3=138). The amount of acceleration ranges from
no appreciable increase in tempo in Songs J3 and J10, to as
much as twelve beats per minute in Song J7.

Accompaniment

The songs are traditionally sung a cappella. Songs J2,
J7, and J10 have guitar accompaniment which follows the
chorus lines so closely (rhythmically and harmonically) that
it is difficult to separate the parts for transcription.

Summary

The jubilee songs are performed by small groups of
singers for an audience and are performed in a folk style
which is opposed to the "art" style of the tradition of the
Fisk Jubilee Singers. While a female singer is sometimes
used with a supporting group of all-male singers, all-female
singing groups are uncommon in the jubilee tradition.

The songs are homogeneous in tonal range, since all

exceed the octave. The melodic level formula, $30^\circ : 29^\circ$, expresses a level difference of -1°. The overall melodic direction of the songs shows a tendency toward level melodic movement; upward and downward internal melodic movement is quite marked. A wide variety of intervals is used, with major seconds and major and minor thirds most characteristic. Major and minor thirds dominate the interval patterns and appear to be of special importance; the repetitive monotone is present in all songs, appearing in a series of as many as fourteen notes, and is of structural importance in the contrasting section of the songs. Descending intervals are employed eleven percent more than are ascending intervals.

Syncopation and the offbeat phrasing of melodic accents are clearly characteristic. The use of ornamental devices such as the rising attack, falling release, rising release, and glissando are common to all songs; in addition, vocal embellishment ranging from two notes per syllable to extreme melismatic patterns (twenty-one notes per syllable) are noted. The songs form a highly homogeneous group in the use of 4/4 meter and a wide range of durational values.

The formal structure of the songs is based upon two principles of construction: (1) leader and chorus overlapping call-and-response pattern, and (2) the alternation of identifying sections, in which melody and verse are rela-

tively fixed, and contrasting sections in which the leader
improvises melody and verse over repeated chorus phrases.
Full harmony is used in all the songs, and while the harmonic
material employed is subject to analysis in terms of the
Western musical system, the manner of usage runs counter
to the technical, and theoretical, practices adhered to in
the religious music of Euroamerican culture. A hypothetical
scale using all of the notes employed in the songs results
in a chromatic scale which encompasses two octaves and a perfect fifth; the scales of individual songs are octo, nona,
and deca, while the modes are penta, hexa, and hepta--two
songs were not susceptible to modal analysis. Although the
slight upward shift in pitch of a semitone is present in
most songs, a strong tonality is maintained in all cases.
Melodic tempi range from 60 to 152 quarter notes per minute,
and acceleration is most songs is slight.

Finally, the jubilee songs are homogeneous in terms of
tonal range, general melodic direction, melodic meter,
melodic usage, harmonic usage, ornamental devices, durational
values, and overall formal structure. They are heterogeneous in tempo, scale, mode, and the organization of phrase
patterns.

Song J2

Song 52

"A" He's al - migh - ty and that is true "B"

He was a ba - by like I or you "C"

is for Christ de - cen - ded from God - - "D"

He was a doc - tor and a man of war "E"

is for the ea - gle with the watch - ful eye - - "F"

is for the fi - re that E - li - jah tried "G"

Song J2

is for God which ev-ry bo-dy knows "H" - - -

He's a hea-ler for the dy-ing soul "I"

He's in-tel-li-gent and He's ver-y wise "J"

He's Je-ho-va for He can-not lie "K" - - - is

for the King I'm pre-pared to say "L" He's

a law-yer and will plead your case "M" is

230.

Song 52

well now "O" is

my Lord is wri -ting all the time

dum dum dum dum dum

for O - me - ga the first and last "P" He's a

Un - Hum Un - Hum

pro -phet just a hold a fast "Q" He's quick

and He is slow "R" ra likes to ride where

no man knows "S" is for the Sa - viour - - - -

232.

Song J2

Song J2

all you say my Lord is wri - ting all the time.

235.

Song J3

Song 53

Song J3

Song J4:96

Song 34

Song J4

Song J4

walk- ing a- bout | well they | asked him where - - -

that his | strength should be | well she | talk

so sweet | and she | talk so fair | well Samp-

-- son told her strength | lie | in his hair

well the | road is migh - ty rug- ged | Oh -

must go

Song J4

well the road is migh- ty rug- ged

must go   must go   and I

well I must go see   my   Lord

must go

Song J5

- and Oh we gon-na ask   Oh Lord He's gon-na
- and - - - - -   ask God in faith - - - - - -

grant - - - - - - - - it   Oh yes we'll tear down con-fus-ion
grant it in grace   tear down con-fus-ion-

in this land   well now you read in the Bi-ble you
in this land in this land (hum) - - - - - - - - - - - - - - - - -

un-der stand Ma - thu-sa-lem was the old-est man he

lived nine hun-dred and six-ty nine he died and got to

Song 35

Samp - son was the strong - est man re - mem - ber way back in an

an - cient time kill three thou - sand of the Phil - is - tine

Samp - son he went walk - ing a - bout Samp - - son's

strength was ne - ver found out un - til his wife sat up - on

his knee ask him where that his strength should be

Song 15

ask - - - - my God in faith He's goin' to | grant yes Oh Lord -

ask God in faith grant it in

- - - - - then we'll tear - down con - fus - ion in this

tear down con - fus - ion in this

land.

land in this land.

Song J6

me - - - - - - - - - - - well - - - you know I'm way - - - - - ay down
- - - a -bout me

here   down   Oh yes - -
in Zi - i - on val - ley my Lord I'm

my Lord - - -   my Lord
my self - -
cross   up - on   my   shoul - der Lord I'm

                        my Lord

have mer - cy from hea - ven   down here I'm pray - ing

come on and   see   a - bout   me
come on and see a - bout see 'bout me.

Song J8

world that I just come from Oh and I looked up

old Da - vid in the heat of the day tuned up

my harp - - - and be - gan to play new

Ba Ba Um Ba new tell me where

Yes - - - well - - -

shall I be - - - - - I'm gon - na be down on my - - knees

- - - - - Lord when it sounds

Hey when my Lord sounds sound that trum - pet Lord.

Song B.

--- His laws up- on mo- - ses ro- ock-- then He give

him com- mand- ments one by one say Mos- es My

will uh must be done now when the first com- mand

doodle

ment my God - - - speaks free do not

oodle loo doodle oodle loo doo

have o- ther Gods be- fore me in the se- -

cond com- mand- ment my God spoke to thee do not

ther and fa - ther too

Yes - - - - - - - Ten com -

Yeh heh - - yeh - -

mand - ments Ten com - mand ments ten com -

well now you

-mand - ments these are the laws of the Lord

honor my God to do His will be -

doodle oodle loo doodle oodle

cause the sixth com-mand-ment says to do not kill do

loo doo

com - mit a - dul - try num - ber sev - en say you

Song J9

Song J9

--- don't you write no more -- be- cause times
that's been won't be no more gon- na close up the
hea- vens door well John was prea- ching to
a nat - ion that had no ci - vi - li - za -- tion
but you read in the Bi - ble says in the gar- den God

Song J10

Song J10

4. Analysis of the Gospel Style

Tonal range

The gospel songs vary in tonal range from twelve semitones, as in Songs G1, G2, G5 and G10, to twenty-four semitones, as in Song G8. In terms of total range they are
rather similar in that they encompass the wide range of an
octave or more.

Melodic level, direction, and contour

The level formula derived from an analysis of crucial
tonal positions is $29^{\circ} : 27^{\circ}$, and expresses a level difference of -2°, thus indicating a surprisingly level melodic
direction for this group of songs.

The character of beginning-ending tone relationships
emphasizes a level direction in overall melodic movement.
In five songs (G1, G5, G6, G7, and G9) these two tones are
identical, in three songs (G2, G3, and G8) the final tone is
from seven to nine semitones below the initial tone, and in
two songs (G10 and G4) the final tone is respectively five
and twelve semitones above the initial tone.

The highest tone is consistently above the initial
tone in a range of from five semitones in Songs G2 and G3,
to nineteen semitones in Song G4.

The relationship between the beginning tone and the
lowest tone is slightly less consistent, but the lowest tone
never exceeds the initial tone. In three songs (G5, G4, and

G10) the initial and lowest tones are identical, while in
all other cases, the lowest tone ranges from three to twelve
semitones below the initial tone.

The ending-lowest tone relationship is similar to the
preceeding tonal relation patterns. In three songs (G2,
G5, and G8) the lowest tone equals the final tone, while in
other cases the lowest tone ranges from five semitones
(Songs G1, G6, G7, and G10) to twelve semitones below (Song
G4) the final tone.

The highest tone is consistently above the ending
tone, ranging from seven semitones above (Songs G1, G4, and
G10) to twenty-four semitones above (Song G8).

Internal melodic movement both upward and downward is
characteristic of this body of song. Upward internal melodic
movement is most strongly marked, since in all cases the
highest tone is above both the initial and final tones. Five
types of melodic contour are created by the variation in
relationship between the critical tones in each song (Fig. 25).

Melodic intervals

Of 593 ascending intervals the major second is most
frequently used (38.1%), followed respectively by the minor
third (26%), major third (15%), perfect fourth (6.1%), minor
second (5.2%), perfect fifth (3.6%), and major sixth (2.3%).
The major seventh, augmented fourth, minor seventh, and
octave and tenth together account for only 2.3% of the total

Fig. 25 DIAGRAM OF MELODIC CONTOUR IN GOSPELS

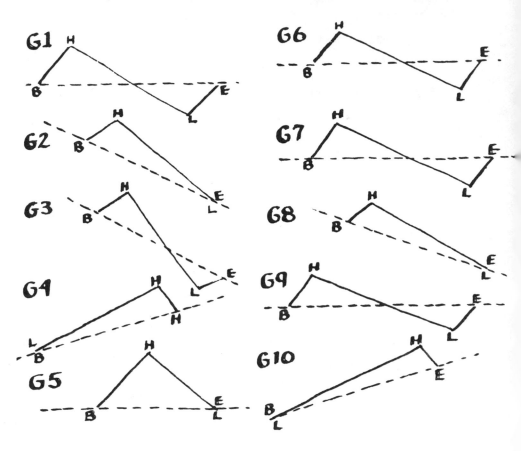

ascending intervals used.

Of 823 descending intervals, the major second is used most frequently (56.1%), followed by the minor third (23.1%), major third (10.1%), minor second (5.5%), perfect fourth (3.4%), and perfect fifth (1.1%). The major sixth and minor seventh account for less than one percent of the total ascending intervals.

Of the total 1416 ascending and descending intervals, the major second is most frequently used (48.5%), followed by the minor third (24.7%), major third (12.1%), minor second (5.4%), perfect fourth (4.5%), perfect fifth (2.1%), and major sixth (1.05%). The augmented fourth, major seventh, minor seventh, octave, and tenth account for less than two percent of the total ascending and descending intervals used.

A wide variety of intervals is employed; of the twelve kinds of intervals used, twelve are used ascending and only nine descending. The major seventh, octave, and tenth are employed ascending but not descending.

Descending intervals account for 58.9% of the total intervals used, while ascending intervals represent 41.1% of the total intervals used. Seventy-six and eight-tenths percent of the intervals used are narrow, 12.9% are medium, and 10.3% are wide.

In terms of melodic interval usage, then, this group of songs is characterized by a wide variety of intervals of which narrow intervals are predominant. Descending intervals are used 17.8% more than ascending intervals and among both ascending and descending intervals the major second is most frequently used (48.5%).

Melodic interval patterns

While major seconds are most frequently used, thirds (major and minor) also appear to be of importance. This

is seen in the triadic split fifth which is of structural
importance in three songs (G4, G8, and G9) which include at
least eight such patterns, and which is found to a lesser
extent in five other songs. Of the forty-three such melodic
interval patterns used in this group of songs, one is diminished rising, eight major rising, fourteen major falling,
ten minor rising, and ten minor falling. Pendular thirds
are found less frequently and in fewer songs (G3, G5, G6, G7,
and G10). Of ten such patterns used, seven are of the
simple type; one Mfrf, two mrfr, four mfrf; and three are
of the extended type, one mrfrf and two mfrfr. The repetitive monotone is found in seven songs (G1, G2, G4, G5, G6,
G7, and G8) in patterns of 4, 5, and 6 notes, and appears to
be of structural importance only in Song G1.

Ornamentation and melodic devices

Ornamental melodic devices are a fundamental characteristic in all of these songs. In addition to the great frequency of glissando, falling release, rising attack, and
rising release, there is a strong concentration by the lead
singer upon improvised patterns of vocal embellishment.
Several patterns of embellishment are used: (1) pendular
minor seconds (Fig. 26), (2) pendular major seconds (Fig. 27),
(3) patterns of thirds and fourths (Fig. 28), and (4) combinations of the above patterns (Figs. 29 and 30).

While the nature of these melismatic patterns is essen-

tially melodic, it may be of value to point out the use of
tones which are foreign to the underlying harmonic structure. In relation to the chords which support them (note
in brackets those tones may be best described as auxiliary

tones (X) and appoggiaturas (AP). (Figs. 26, 27, 29, and 30)

Syncopation and the offbeat phrasing of melodic accents
are prominent features in gospel songs. The points of
rhythmic stress vary, as do durational values, with individual phrases in the melodic line, and there is a characteristic avoidance of placing accents with mechanical regularity as is done in the Western church music tradition.
Special attention may be given (Fig. 31) to the shifting of
the phrase "There's a man on the over side," as it is repeated as well as to changes in durational values in the
repetition of the phrase "I wanna go there." The melodic

rhythm of the leader's phrases is, however, only one facet of the total rhythmic scheme found in these songs. A larger, more inclusive pattern is formed by the interaction of leader and chorus phrases; this point will be dealt with in our discussion of harmonic rhythm.

Melodic meter and durational values

Leader and chorus lines are sung in the same meter in all songs, four of which are in 6/8 and five in 4/4; one song could not be notated in a strict metric formula. The latter is not uncommon to the "soul-singing" of soloists (but not groups of gospel singers) when performing songs at a slow tempo and includes a good deal of melodic embellishment; the free metric structure is apparently designed to allow the singer ample liberty to improvise without temporal restriction.

Of the fourteen kinds of durational values used, the sixteenth note appears most frequently (35.2%), followed by the eighth note (25.6%), quarter note (12.2%), thirty-second note (6.4%), dotted eighth note (6.4%), dotted quarter note (5.1%), triplet sixteenth note (3.1%), half note (2.2%), and dotted sixteenth note tied to a quarter note (1.1%). The dotted half note, whole note, triplet eighth note, and eighth note tied to a half note account for 1.4% of the total kinds of durational values. Thus, a wide variety of durational values is characteristic of this group of songs.

Formal structure

The overall formal structure of the gospel songs is
fundamentally based upon the overlapping leader-chorus call-
and-response pattern (the overlapping rarely exceeds two
beats) which is present in all songs with the exception of
the solos. An additional principle of construction, frequently used in alternation with the call-and-response pattern, is the inclusion of a kind of introductory section (as
in Songs G4, G5, G6, G7, and G9) in which either leader or
chorus does not sing. There is variation in the employment
of the second principle, since the "verse" section it creates
varies in length and in its position in the performance.
In Song G8, for example, it is sung by the chorus, and is only
eight measures in length; in Songs G4 and G5, it is sung by
the leader and encompasses thirty-two bars; and, in Song
G6 it is eight measures long and returns to the main melody.

The leader (A) and chorus (B) patterning shows more
regularity in that it is consistently of the short phrase
overlapping call-and-response type. Both leader and chorus
phrases show a complex pattern of sub-phrases. The leader's
phrases are complex and show variation in both melodic content and durational values, while the chorus phrases change
harmonically but show less rhythmic variation, tending to
be rhythmically repetitious.

Harmony and harmonic rhythm

Harmony, as utilized in this style, has great similarity

to the harmonic concept used in the Jubilee songs. However,
the use of instrumental accompaniment in the gospel style
has affected the leader-chorus relationship to the degree
that the function of chorus phrases as a harmonic base for
the melodic phrases of the leader is of less importance
here than in the Jubilee style. The interaction of chorus
and leader phrases forms a strict short-phrase overlapping
call-and-response pattern, and the harmonic phrases sung by
the chorus tend to have strong melodic individuality in
addition to rhythmic and harmonic interest. Indeed, the
chorus phrases can be conceived as creating subordinate
melodic material which complements the leader's phrases.
Note, for example, the exchange of phrases between leader
and chorus in Songs G6 and G7 (Fig. 32).

In addition to supplying subordinate melodic material,
the harmonic rhythm of the chorus complements the melodic
rhythm of the leader's phrases and keeps the overall rhythmic
pattern of the vocal lines flowing. Note, for example, how
the chorus phrases fill the rhythmic gaps left when the
leader drops out in Song G8 (Fig. 33).

Other harmonic usages found in the gospel style include
the use of six-four chords in series (Fig. 34), incomplete
chords due to the doubling of tones or the dropping out of
a voice (Fig. 35), and supertonic harmony, without the seventh
of the chord, as a substitute for subdominant harmony in the
cadence (Fig. 36).

In summary, the basic chords found in the Western musical
system are utilized, but harmonic usage which is usually
avoided in the Euroamerican hymn song tradition is common
in the gospel style. Further, the harmonic phrases of the
chorus are of less importance as a background for melody
than in the jubilee tradition and tend to have a large measure
of the melodic individuality.

Scale, mode, duration tone, and subjective tonic

A hypothetical scale using all of the tones appearing
in these songs results in a chromatic scale which ranges
two octaves and a perfect fifth. Observing the scales formed
by using the number of tones employed in each song, not
counting octaves, one song is deca, one hexa, one hepta,
three nona and four octo. In terms of mode, three songs are
pentatonic, two hexatonic, and four use some type of hepta
mode. The penta structures are all of the normal penta do
type, 5:5:1; likewise, the hexa structures are normal hexa
do, 6:6:1. Of the hepta structures, one is hepta sol,
7:7:5, one hepta do, 7:7:1 and two hepta do, but using less
than seven tones to form a 6:7:1 structure. Song G1 was not

susceptible to modal analysis due to its chromatic character. Modally, then, these songs do not represent a homogeneous grouping (see appendix).

A strongly established tonality is maintained in all of the songs, apparently with the aid of instrumental accompaniment, and with no cases of modulation. The duration tone and subjective tonic fall on the same pitch in nine of the songs, and in the remaining song the duration tone falls on the fifth degree of the subjective tonic scale.

Tempo

Melodic tempi in the gospel songs, based upon the quarter note, range from 56 to 138 beats per minute. The slower tempi (56, 62, 64, and 90) are found in 6/8, while the tempi in 4/4 are faster and have a wider range (84, 104, 108, 126, and 138). The amount of acceleration ranges from no appreciable increase in tempo in Song G2 as much as fourteen beats per minute in Song G1.

Accompaniment

Gospel singing is always accompanied by musical instruments, and most characteristically by piano and organ, either together or separately; sometimes this instrumental arrangement is supplemented by a tambourine, saxophone, or trombone. Three techniques of accompaniment on keyboard instruments are observable: an overlapping call-and-response pattern (Fig. 37); a pattern in which the basic beat is established

in the bass in octave patterns (left-hand) while improvised octave and chord patterns are played above (right-
hand), (Fig. 38), and a pattern in which inner tones move
against stationary tones in upper and lower positions
(Fig. 39).

The harmonic content of instrumental accompaniment in this style is susceptible to analysis in terms of the Western musical system; however, many chord progressions and structures which are typical of gospel accompaniment are usually avoided in Western church music (Fig. 40).

Instrumental accompaniment, traditionally uncommon
to both the spiritual and jubilee styles, is an integral
part of the performance of gospel songs; however,
accompaniment here (as we shall later see) is not performed strictly as written; improvisation is a chief
characteristic.

Written music and musical performance

As noted above (p. 124), although gospel music has been
subjected to a written form, the printed music serves only
as a guide to the performance of the music. In an apparent
response to the tradition of free interpretation, liberties
are taken with harmony, melody, rhythm, and meter. The
melodic and rhythmic phrases of the leaders' lines are never
sung strictly as written (Figs. 41 and 42), and the harmonies
sung by the chorus are frequently embellished with passing
tones (Figs. 43 and 44). Songs written in one meter are
often adapted to another, as for example, with Songs G7 and
G10 (Figs. 42 and 43) in which the meter is changed from 3/4
to 8/8; Song G2 (Fig. 41) in which the meter is changed from
3/4 to 4/4; and Song G9 (Fig. 44) in which the meter is
changed from 4/4 to 6/8. In extreme cases, as in the performance of Song G3 (Fig. 45) a free metrical structure is
employed. Freedom of interpretation is simi   characteristic of accompaniment, for which there frequently is no
specially written part (Figs. 46 and 47).

Summary

Gospel songs are performed by small groups (Songs G4, G5, G8, and G9), choirs (Songs G1 and G6) and soloists (Songs G10, G2, and G3).

The songs analyzed here are rather similar in terms of tonal range since they encompass the wide range of an octave or more. The melodic level formula $29^{\circ} : 27^{\circ}$ expresses a level difference of -2°. A slightly level direction in overall melodic movement and upward and downward internal melodic movement are characteristic of this group of songs. The wide variety of intervals used is dominated by narrow intervals, and the major second is used most frequently (48.5%) of all intervals, ascending and descending. Major and minor thirds dominate the interval patterns, and the repetitive monotone, which appears in series of 4, 5, and 6 notes, is structurally important in only one song (G1). Descending intervals are employed 17.8% more than ascending intervals.

Syncopation and the offbeat phrasing of melodic accents are strongly marked features. Ornamental melodic devices are fundamental and the rising attack, falling release, and glissando are supplemented by patterns of improvised vocal embellishment. Six/eight and 4/4 are the commonly used meters; one song is not metrically structured. A wide range of durational values is used and the sixteenth note appears most frequently.

The overall formal structure of the songs is based
upon the overlapping leader-chorus call-and-response
pattern; frequently an additional principle of construction,
in which a "verse" section alternates with call-and-response
patterning, is employed. Full harmony is used, and the
chords are structurally similar to the chords used in the
Jubilee style, although harmonic phrases serve less as a
base for the melodic lines of the leader and tend to have
strong melodic individuality, as well as rhythm and harmonic
interest. The harmonic materials used diverge from the
practices common to Western church music. A hypothetical
scale using all of the notes employed in the songs creates
a chromatic scale which encompasses two octaves and a perfect fifth. The scales of the various songs are deca, nona,
octo, hepta, and hexa. The modal structures are penta, hepta,
and hexa; one song is not susceptible to modal analysis.
A strongly established tonality, aided by instrumental accompaniment, is maintained, and the duration tone and subjective
tonic fall on the same pitch with one exception. Melodic
tempi range from 56 to 138 beats per minute based upon the
quarter note; the slower tempi (56 to 80) are found in 6/8
time. Instrumental accompaniment, in which the piano and
organ are used, is fundamental to the performance of the
songs. Performance, in both its vocal and instrumental
aspects, avoids strict adherence to printed music, and

individual interpretation and improvisation are characteristic of leader phrases and instrumental accompaniment.

Finally, the gospel songs are homogeneous in tonal range, general melodic direction, melodic interval usage, use of ornamental devices, melodic meter, durational values, overall formal structure, harmonic usage, accompaniment patterns, and stress upon individual interpretation. They are heterogeneous in scale, mode, and the organization of phrase patterns.

Song 62:3u:154-168

Song G3

in - - - - - - - - pray - - - - - - er.

Song 64: 3u:112   325.

(leader) Since I met Je - ee - ee - ee - su - us

lo - - - - er - - erd   there's a bur - - - - - ur - ning   Oh

such a bur - ning   deep down with - in - - - - - -

don't you know that it holds - - me   with an un - seen

pow - ow - ow   ow - er - er - er   and it keeps me

free from all si - i - in   it chan - ges

me - ee - ee   from day - ay - - - - to day   as I

walk - - a - lon - on - ong   this na - a - a - a

arrow   wa - ay   since I - - - - met   Je - ee - - - ee - sus

- - - since He blessed this whole - - - soul   of

Song G5:5u:104

(leader) I know the Lor - - - ord will make a way-ay

yes He will I know the Lord

will make a way-ay yes He will - - -

He will make a way for you and He'll

lead - - you safe-ly through I know the Lord - -

will make a way-ay - - - - yes He will

I have a sav-iour I can tell all - -

- - - - - - - - my trou-bles to when I'm

bur-dened and I don't know Ju - ust what to

do I - just run to God - - - in

Song G5

se - cret pra- ayer He told me I could le -eave all of my bur - dens there I - - -know thew Lord - - He'll make a way - - - yes He will Oh - - - yes He will - . . . Oh yes He will - - - Yes He will yes He will - - - yes He will yes He will yes He will - - - yes He will Oh - - yes He - - . . will I tell you I'm a wit - ness Yes He will yes He will Yes He will

Song G5

that He will .... I --

yes He will yes He will yes He will

know the Lord .... sure will make a way

I know the Lord will make

Oh yes He will - I tell you

way Oh yes He will ----

some-times I feel like I have-n't got a friend

some times yes yes yes yes yes

but He prom-ised to go with me un - - -

yes yes yes yes

Song G6

hap - py day.

hap - py day.

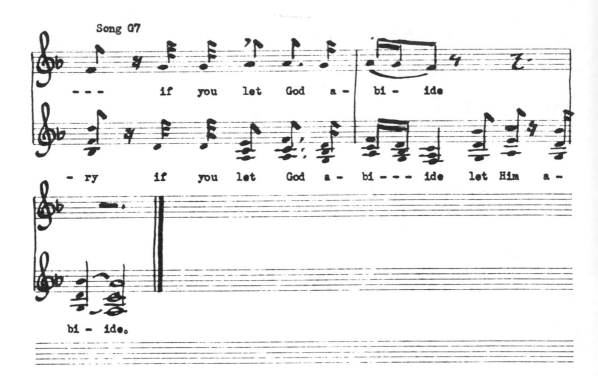

Song Q7

--- if you let God a - bi - ide

- ry if you let God a - bi --- ide let Him a -

bi - ide.

Song G8:3u:84

I got a tel - le - phone in my bos - om and

I can ring Him up from my heart I got a

tel - le - phone in my bo - som and I can ring him

I know Je- sus is on the

up from my heart

ma - ain li — i -ine

tell Him what you want

Song 68

Je - su- u - us is
tell Him what you want
on the main li - i - ine
tell Him what you
I say Je - sus is on the ma - ain
want
li - i - ine
tell Him what you
tell Him what you want
want
ca- all Him up uh - up
tell Him what you want
call Him

Song G8

Song 06

ant ---

Him   wha - at   you   wa - ant.

Song G9

but I don't mind   just

-- don't mind   I --- don't mind

so- I-------- reach   my heaven-ly home-

so------- I reach   reach-

--......   -- my hea-ea-ven-ly ho--me.

Song GlO:ld:56

Just one tou --- ouch as He mo-oo- 'oo-

moved a long He was pushed He was pre------

essed by a jo-o----------ost-ling throng

ju--------------ust just one touch and

the weak was made stro--ong I I've been

saved by His pow--er--- er------ di-

vine Oh--- Oh---- Oh saved by His pow---

ow-er di-vi-i-i-i-------------- ine

I'm saved by His pow- ow- wer- er

di-vine--- Oh Oh------- Oh glo-ry----

Song Al:3u:154

Song A2

Song A5:80

VI. COMPARISON OF MUSICAL STYLE

From the quantitative descriptions of the existing
forms in the religious music of the United States Negro
presented in the preceding chapter, comparison, in precise terms, is possible. Such comparison makes two other
aims of this study possible by (1) providing criteria for
establishing the relationships between three styles considered, and (2) defining the gospel style based upon its
differentiation from the other forms in the tradition. If
the postulate of close correspondence among the three
styles holds true, we should discover (1) a large number
of shared characteri tics among the three styles and (2)
closer correspondence between gospel and jubilee songs
than between gospel and spiritual songs.

In melodic direction, gospel and jubilee songs show
a close similarity because of their level character, while
the spirituals show a marked downward movement in melodic
direction. These characteristics are clearly shown in
level differences (Table 7), the beginning-ending tone
relationships (Table 7), and the diagrams of melodic direction (Fig. 48).

The three groups of songs are similar in the percentage of ascending and descending intervals used

TABLE 7. COMPARISON OF TONAL RELATIONS AND LEVEL DIFFERENCES

	Spiritual	Jubilee	Gospel
Ending tone equal to lowest tone	3	2	5
Ending tone above lowest tone	7	8	5
Beginning tone equal to ending tone	3	6	5
Beginning tone above ending tone	7	2	2
Beginning tone below ending tone			
Level difference	-29°	-1°	-2°

Fig. 48 COMPARISON OF MELODIC CONTOUR

Spiritual Jubilee Gospel

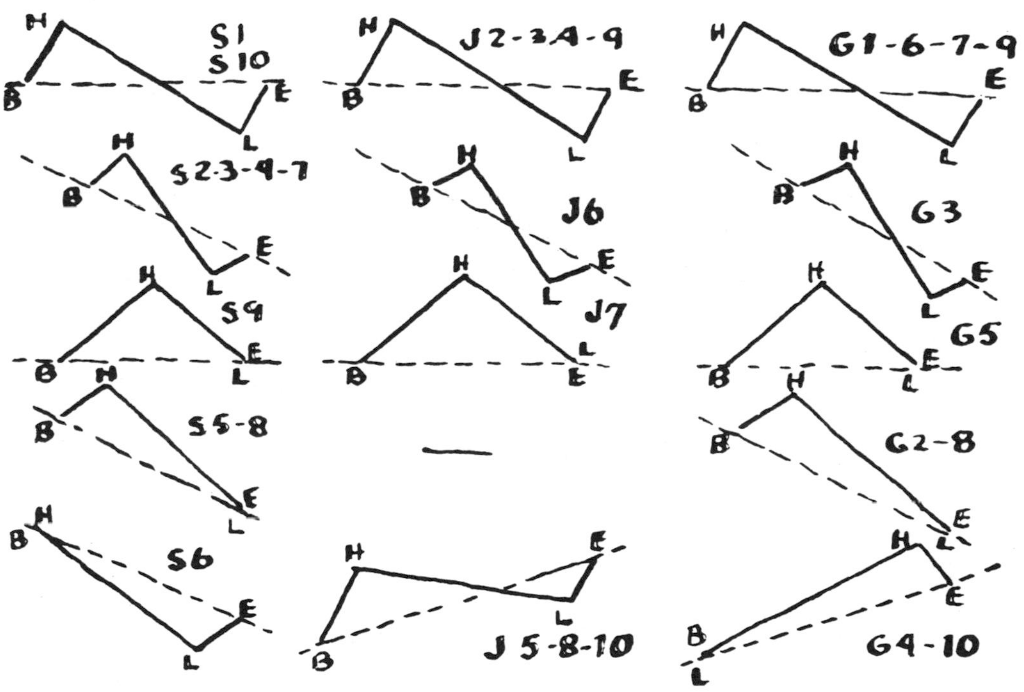

(Table 8), and in the use of a small percentage of wide
intervals (Table 8), but the gospel songs show a higher percentage of narrow intervals (Table 8) and a smaller percentage of medium intervals than the spiritual and jubilee
songs (Table 8). While the jubilee songs use a higher
percentage of minor seconds than spiritual and gospel songs,
the gospel songs differ clearly from jubilees and spirituals
in greater use of major seconds and less use of major
thirds (Table 9). All three songs are closely similar in
the percentage of minor thirds used.

TABLE 8. COMPARISON OF INTERVALS

	Spirituals	Jubilees	Gospel
Narrow intervals	65.2%	64.5%	76.8%
Medium intervals	24 %	19.4%	10.3%
Wide intervals	10.8%	16.1%	12.9%
Total ascending intervals	44.1%	44.5%	41.1%
Total descending intervals	55.9%	55.5%	58.9%

Frequent use is made of triadic split fifths in all
three groups of songs--especially the split major structure
in spirituals and jubilees and split minor structures in
gospels (Table 10). Spirituals make more frequent use of
pendular thirds than do jubilees or gospels, but while gospels make less use of these pendular patterns than either
spirituals or jubilees (Table 10), the repetitive monotone

TABLE 9.   COMPARISON OF INTERVAL USAGE

	Spiritual	Jubilee	Gospel
Ascending intervals			
Minor second	9.6%	14.8%	5.2%
Major second	32.4%	25.5%	38.1%
Minor third	20.1%	24.8%	26.0%
Major third	24.6%	22.9%	15.0%
Perfect fourth	7.1%	10.3%	6.0%
Perfect fifth	3.0%	---	3.6%
Major sixth	---	---	2.3%
Descending intervals			
Minor second	9.4%	14.0%	5.5%
Major second	37.8%	29.6%	56.1%
Minor third	20.6%	23.3%	23.1%
Major third	23.7%	18.4%	10.8%
Perfect fourth	6.1%	7.0%	3.4%
Perfect fifth	---	4.0%	1.0%
Octave	---	1.4%	---
Total intervals			
Minor second	9.4%	14.2%	5.4%
Major second	35.4%	27.9%	48.5%
Minor third	20.6%	23.9%	24.7%
Major third	24.0%	20.4%	12.1%
Perfect fourth	6.9%	8.0%	4.5%
Perfect fifth	1.8%	3.0%	2.1%
Octave	---	1.0%	---

TABLE 10. COMPARISON OF INTERVAL PATTERNS

	Spiritual No. of songs	Spiritual No. of patterns	Jubilee No. of songs	Jubilee No. of patterns	Gospel No. of songs	Gospel No. of patterns
Split diminished triad	1	4	2	2	1	1
Split major triad	6	28 ⎱ 42	7	23 ⎱ 32	7	21 ⎱ 42
Split minor triad	3	10 ⎰	3	7 ⎰	8	20 ⎰
Pendular major thirds	5	38 ⎱ 42	6	10 ⎱ 18	1	1 ⎱ 10
Pendular minor thirds	3	3 ⎰	4	8 ⎰	5	9 ⎰
Fourths rf	4	6 ⎱ 11	1	2 ⎱ 11	-	-
Fourths fr	2	5 ⎰	5	8 ⎰	-	-
Octaves	-	-	2	2	-	-
Repetitive monotone	10 (4 to 9 notes per pattern)		10 (4 to 14 notes per pattern)		7 (4 to 6 notes per pattern)	

pattern is frequently used in the three bodies of song, but appears less clearly marked in the gospel songs (Table 10).

The songs in all three groups have a wide tonal range, and the ranges of the jubilees and gospels are wider than the ranges found among the spirituals. However, the range distribution among the gospel songs shows similarity both to the spirituals and jubilees in that the ranges of the largest number of songs cluster around 12-14 semitones (as in the spirituals) while a smaller number of songs show a wider total tonal range as in the case of the jubilees (Table 11).

TABLE 11. COMPARISON OF TONAL RANGE

(Total tonal range)	Spiritual (8 - 16)	Jubilee (14 - 26)	Gospel (12 - 24)
Range in semitones			
8			
9			
10			
11			
12	4		4
13			
14	4	1	2
15		1	
16	1	2	
17		3	1
18			
19			1
20			1
21		1	
22		1	
23			
24			1
25			
26		1	

The three song groups are highly similar in their use
of penta, hexa, and hepta modal structures and the use of
chromatic tones which make some songs not susceptible of
modal analysis (Table 12). In scale structures, the gospel
song group shows similarity both to spiritual and jubilee
songs. In all three song groups the relation between the
duration tone and subjective tonic is direct in most cases
(Table 12).

TABLE 12. COMPARISON OF MODE, SCALE, AND DURATION
TONE

	Spiritual	Jubilee	Gospel
Mode:	Penta-3	Penta-2	Penta-3
	Hexa-2	Hexa-2	Hexa-2
	Hepta-4	Hepta-4	Hepta-4
	Not susceptible of analysis - 1	Not susceptible of analysis-2	Not susceptible of analysis-1
Scale:	Hexa-2		Hexa-1
	Hepta-3		Hepta-1
	Octo-4	Octo-2	Octo-4
	Nona-1	Nona-3	Nona-3
		Deca-5	Deca-1
Number of songs in which duration tone and subjective tonic are equal	9	8	9

All three song groups are marked by the consistent use
of the overlapping call-and-response pattern. Wide use of
ornamental melodic devices is similarly a common characteristic and appears to have increased complexity as used in the
jubilee and gospel songs (Fig. 49). Stress on improvisation

in the leader's lines is also commonly shared, as is syncopation and the offbeat phrasing of melodic accents (Fig. 50).

The harmony found in spirituals is created incidentally by the overlapping of leader and chorus phrases (Fig. 51). The use of full-harmony is characteristic of both jubilee and gospel songs, and while the harmonic vocabulary of these song groups may be expressed in terms of the Western musical

Fig. 51

Song S6

(chorus) ev-ry bo- dy talk a - bout hea- ver ain't goin' there ETC

(leader)

- ry bo- dy talk a- bout hea- ven ain't goin' there

Song J2

(leader) Well you read in your Bi- ble read it well you ETC

(chorus) (Hum)

Song G7

(leader) with-in your soul Oh Lord deep down with - ETC

(chorus)

with - in . your soul

system, their manner of harmonic usage is usually avoided in the Euroamerican hymn song tradition. In contrast to jubilee songs, harmonic phrases in gospel songs are of less impor- tance as a background for melody and tend to show melodic individuality in forming harmonized subordinate melodic

material which follows the leader's melodic lines in an overlapping call-and-response pattern (Fig. 51).

In the case of gospel songs, instrumental accompaniment
is a characteristic part of musical performance, and in this
respect, gospel songs stand clearly apart from the jubilees
and spirituals. Printed music is similarly peculiar to gospel
songs, although under the force of the tradition of improvisation the music is never performed exactly as written in
either its vocal or instrumental aspects.

Direct relationship among the three styles of religious
music is evident when their considerable number of shared
characteristics is taken into account. Close correlations
among spirituals, jubilees and gospels are seen in the percent
of ascending and descending intervals used (Fig. 45), use of
triadic split fifth (Fig. 47), modal structures employed
(Fig. 49), relation between subjective tonic and the duration
tone (Fig. 49), use of the repetitive monotone pattern,
emphasis on syncopation and the off beat phrasing of melodic
accents (Fig. 51), the importance of the overlapping call-
and-response pattern, and the prominence of improvisation.

The use of instrumental accompaniment is the most marked
characteristic of the gospel style, since it is the only
musical trait not shared to some degree with the other two
styles. However, gospels also show a high degree of differentiation from spirituals and jubilees in greater emphasis

on the use of narrow intervals (Fig. 45), major seconds (Fig.
46), and minor triadic fifths (Fig. 47), less use of major
thirds (Fig. 46), and the unimportance of harmonic phrases
as a background for melody. In characteristics not related
to musical structure, gospels differ distinctly from spirituals and jubiless in the tradition of printed music and the
nature of communication. In the latter respect, spirituals
are traditionally performed in congregational fashion, and
jubiless are sung by small performing groups; gospels,
however, are communicated to an audience by soloists, small
groups, and choirs.

VII. SUMARY AND CONCLUSIONS

The non-historical statistical data, obtained through musicological analysis of the musical samples, show a clear relationship between the various styles of religious music under consideration and point to the retention, in the contemporary style, of structural musical characteristics which are basic to the religious tradition in United States Negro music.

Ethnographic and historical data have, in addition, provided insight into the processes through which African musical values were retained, and reinterpretation has provided for the smooth integration of new elements into the United States Negro's culturally sanctioned musical patterns and values. Cultural patterns and values important as part of the religious complex of the indigenous African cultural heritage, were retained by the United States Negro, even under the conditions of slavery. In spite of restrictions and precautions against all-Negro religious meetings and the proselyting by various Western churches, the enslaved Negro managed to practice his own religion in his own way; and traditional religious values and practices, such as the importance and form of baptism and possession, were preserved through the mechanism of reinterpretation. The musical concept employed in this religious complex was also tenacious,

and though subject to some restrictions (primarily the use
of percussion instruments) and Euroamerican influence, African
musical patterns and values are found (1) in the strong
rhythmic characteristics, (2) in the close relation of the
songs to dancing (religious) and other forms of bodily
activity, (3) in the importance of improvisation in the
melodic lines of the leader, (4) in patterns of interaction
between leader and chorus in the performance of the songs,
and (5) in the honor and esteem accorded a good song leader.

The retention of African musical values was aided by
the facts that (1) music was not the object of total suppression during slavery; (2) musical culture is carried below
the level of consciousness and is not dependent upon social
or ecological setting for survival; and (3) the compatibility
of African and Euroamerican musical systems permitted reciprocal cultural exchange and reinterpretation in adjacent musical
forms. The influence of the Euroamerican hymn-song tradition upon United States Negro religious music is indicated
by various studies (White 1928; Jackson 1943), but the whole
question of the extent or the influence of white spirituals
upon Negro spirituals must remain an academic problem until
sufficient data for analysis and comparison are available.

Indeed, a strong case can be argued for the influence
of African music values upon the Euroamerican tradition;
this is clearly seen in the area of secular music (i.e.,

minstrel songs, Stephen Foster type plantation songs) and
indicates the reciprocal exchange of musical culture which
the anthropologist views as commonplace, but which is not
clearly understood by those students who deny the possibility
of such an occurrence in the area of sacred music. Thus,
extreme caution must be exercised in positing generalizations
concerning the dominance of Euroamerican music over African
musical tradition in the early period of culture contact
in the United States.[1] The retention of African musical values
is, however, quite apparent in the United States Negro
spiritual style, and for the student of culture (since the
characteristics of the Western musical tradition are available) collection of data relative to the structural characteristics of African and United States Negro musical styles
is the most important step toward a total assessment of
cultural accommodation and integration in United States
Negro music.

The jubilee style of untrained Negro singers appeared
after Emancipation and was influenced by the art forms of
Negro religious music which grew out of the tradition of

[1]This problem is not always treated with the caution
demanded. One of the prominent studies (Jackson 1943) which
is designed to show the dominant influence of white spirituals
upon Negro spirituals suffers from the fact that the musical
examples had been treated so as to eliminate such fundamental characteristics of the Negro style as vocal embellishments, the call-and-response pattern, and overlapping.
Further, the tradition of improvisation, so basic to the
Negro musical tradition is completely ignored in the versions
of the Negro songs used.

the tradition of harmonized and arranged spirituals performed
by choirs of educated Negroes. The tradition of performing
groups (as opposed to congregational singing) and the use of
full harmony were incorporated into the folk tradition, but
not without experiencing a reworking of pre-established
musical patterns and values. The background for acceptance
of the patterns of performing groups of singers is seen in
the tradition of "basing," in which a group of singers stands
aside and provides singing and handclapping as "shouters"
perform their religious dances. Further, the performances
of these singing groups is in essence an imitation or modified version of the leader-chorus pattern traditionally performed by the total congregation. The audience, to a large
extent, shares vicariously in the performance, but as
excitement increases individuals actually begin to "shout"
(dance) and the performing groups then function as "basers."

In the jubilee style, full harmony is not used in strict
homophonic idiom of Western church music, wherein harmony
and melody are sung simultaneously as parts of the same
chord. Instead, the use of full harmony in this folk idiom
is influenced by the pre-existing interest in rhythm, improvisation, and leader-chorus patterning. The harmonic phrases
of the chorus, as used in the contrasting sections of the
jubilee songs, are percussive-like and their rhythmic patterns
heighten the effect of the offbeat phrasing of the leader's
improvised melodic lines.

Spirituals continued as a part of the religious complex of the large body of southern rural Negroes who freely expanded their religious activities, and it was the harmonized and arranged versions of this early form that educated jubilee choirs (i.e., Fisk Jubilee Singers) performed. The folk jubilee singers, however, performed in small groups of from four to six singers (as opposed to whole congregations or choirs) and devloped a song form which incorporated the song-narrative with a standard refrain. This jubilee song-form has earlier been described as having an identifying section (standardized refrain), which employs relatively fixed melody and verse, and a contrasting section in which the leader improvises words and melody over the repetitive harmonized rhythmic pattern of the chorus, and, as we shall see later, it is an innovation in leader-chorus patterning.

The gospel style of United States religious music was developed within the culturally conservative low status group which transplanted southern rural Negro culture to an urban setting. With religion as a focus of interest they produced variations and modifications of the fundamentalist beliefs and practices that were developed during slavery and intensified during the post-Civil War period. Music remained an integral part of this religious complex, and the continuity of religious musical tradition is seen in the use of melodies from the spiritual tradition, full

harmony, techniques of improvisation, and patterns of vocal
embellishment--all found in the jubilee style and easily adapted
to the gospel style.

The musical tradition was similarly the object of experimentation, and the freedom of expression that characterized the religious behavior of the "shouting" churches was
expressed in musical terms. The use of musical instruments
was not characteristic of either the spiritual or jubilee
traditions, due to the restrictions on the use of drums during
slavery and subsequent religious taboos on the use of "worldly"
instruments (piano, organ, violin). However, the principle
of free religious expression combined with a larger economic
base, due to the improved occupational status of Negroes in
the cities, opened the door for the use of such instruments
as piano and organ in the gospel style.

Indeed, one of the most characteristic features of the
gospel style is instrumental accompaniment. The style of
piano and organ accompaniment is, however, different from
that used in the art-form tradition of Negro religious music
or the Euroamerican hymn-song tradition, both of which are
conceived in terms of formal music theory and played strictly
as written. Under the influence of culturally sanctioned
patterns and values, instrumental accompaniment here lays
stress upon improvisation and exhibits a preoccupation with
rhythmic patterns.

Because of its harmonic and intensely rhythmic character, instrumental accompaniment in the gospel style has influenced the use of an additional technique of leader-chorus
patterning. The spiritual style employs a strict overlapping
call-and-response pattern, in which leader and chorus exchange phrases with different melodic and verse content, and
a song has its existence in the connection of these phrases
(Fig. 52).

The jubilee style employs the above technique and, in
addition, uses a characteristic technique wherein melody
and verse are not fragmented but the leader carries the
entire melody over harmonized rhythmic patterns sung by the
chorus, as in the contrasting sections (Fig. 53).

While the gospel style sometimes employs the techniques
found in the spiritual and jubilee styles, it most characteristically uses the overlapping call-and-response pattern
in which the leader sings the entire verse lines, with
improvised melody, while the chorus echoes his phrases with
a harmonized subordinate melody; the instrumental accompaniment provides a continuous harmonic and rhythmic background for this interplay between leader and chorus (Fig. 54).

This observed continuity of musical traditions is a
facet of the complex of behavior and values found among the
large body of culturally conservative Negroes in the United
States. Variation in acculturative experience has resulted
in different rates of change among members of the United
States Negro population. Rapid acculturation is seen in the
case of those who (as early as Colonial times) enjoyed free
access to Western culture and have exhibited an ability to
absorb it and make it a part of family and group tradition.
On the other hand, those whose access to the dominant culture

was limited in pre- and post-Emancipation times have maintained a conservative attitude toward culture change, thus demonstrating that under favorable conditions, previously acquired culture patterns tend to be retained and new items of culture are accepted and modified in terms of pre-existing values and sanctions.

Due to the conditions of slavery in the United States, the largest portion of Negroes were illiterate inhabitants of rural southern areas whose participation in the national culture was greatly restricted and whose cultural behavior and values were thus largely influenced by their pre-American past. Following Emancipation, except for freedom from chattel slavery, their economic and social condition (as well as geographic location) remained essentially unchanged. For more than a century, then, the largest portion of the Negro population was found in a socio-cultural milieu which offered little opportunity for rapid acculturation, but, indeed, made possible continued degrees of retention and reinterpretation of surviving African cultural behavior and values.

When southern rural Negroes started to migrate to urban areas on a large scale, their cultural difference from urbanized Negroes was brought into sharp focus. Social class distinctions among Negroes, based upon cultural differences, resulted in the social isolation of exponents of southern Negro culture and the development of in-group

solidarity among them. This in turn tended to reinforce
their southern rural cultural tradition, and this is most
noticeable in the focal area of religious belief and practice and concomitant musical tradition.

Thus, in support of the postulate of a correlation
between social class, church affiliation, and religious
musical tradition, ethnographic data reveals social class
distinctions among the various religious denominations in
urban Negro communities; further, denominational affiliation is seen to denote commitment to a particular tradition
of religious belief and behavior, and the concomitant tradition of religious music. The Negro upper classes are largely
identified with Euroamerican religious denominations (i.e.,
Episcopal, Congregational) and their doctrine, practice and
musical tradition; Negro middle classes are identified with
large well-established churches of United States Negro
denomination which are characterized by a mixture of Euroamerican and United States Negro patterns of religious behavior, belief, and hymn-song tradition; while the lower
classes are identified largely with the shouting" churches
whose belief and behavior demonstrate the retention and
development of the Negro "old-time" religious tradition and
its accompanying musical aspect.

Finally, in answer to the question as to whether the
contemporary gospel style has shifted away from basic values

of the folk tradition in United States Negro religious music,
by means of a combination of methods (ethno-historical and
ethnomusicological), a direct relationship in terms of
structural characteristics, a relative dating in time, and a
continuity of musical values and practices have been established for the spiritual, jubilee, and gospel styles.
Further, it has been possible to observe the long-term
creative process which has culminated in a contemporary musical style (gospel) that has smoothly integrated the use of
instrumental accompaniment (European musical instruments),
full harmony, and a tradition of performing groups, while
maintaining basic patterns and values of the African musical
tradition.

BIBLIOGRAPHY

Abdy, Edward S.
  1835   Journal of a residence and tour in the
                  United States of North America. London,
                  J. Murray.

Allen, C. G.
  1927   The Negro's contribution to American
                  music.
                  Current History 27:245-49.

Allen, P. L.
  1904   Negro churches. Nation 78:405-06.

Allen, Richard
  n.d.   The life, experience, and gospel labors
                  of the Rt. Reverend Richard Allen to
                  which is annexed the rise and progress
                  of the African Methodist church in the
                  United States of America. Philadelphia,
                  A.M.E. Book Concern.

Allen, W. F.,   C. F. Ware and L. M. Garrison
  1867   Slave songs of the United States.
                  New York, A. Simpson and Company.

Anderson, Robert
  1927   From slavery to affluence. Hemingsford,
                  Nebraska, The Hemingsford Ledger.

Anon
  1866   Education of the freedmen. De Bows
                  Review, New Series 2:95.
  1867a   Georgia. New York Tribune (January 1,
                  1867) 2:1.
  1867b   Reconstruction. New York Tribune
                  (March 26, 1867) 2:1.
  1869   Through the South. New York Tribune
                  (June 30, 1869) 2:1.
  1870   Education in Texas and Louisiana.
                  New York Tribune (May 6, 1870) 2:1.
  1872   The rice Negro as an elector.
                  Nation 15:22-23.
  1874   Sorcery among Negros. New York Times
                  (December 20, 1874) 6:4.

Anon
    1877   (no title) Baptist Home Mission Monthly
                      (August, 1878) 56.
    1881   Life in the Old Dominion. New York
                      Tribune (February 8, 1881) 2:5.
    1887   The Maryland Negroes. New York Times
                      (September 18, 1887) 2:5.
    1890   A watch-night meeting. The American
                      Missionary.44:82-84.
    1914   Negro music in the land of Freedom
                      Outlook 106:611-12.
    1956   Negro migrants in Chicago. Chicago
                      Daily News (March 9, 1956) 1:1.

Armstrong, M. F. and H. W. Ludlow
    1875   Hampton and its students. New York,
                      G. P. Putnam's Sons.

Austin, Mary
    1925   Everyman's genius. Indianapolis, Bobbs-
                      Merrill.

Avary, Myrta L.
    1906   Dixie after the war. New York, D. Appleton
                      and Company.

Baker, Theodor
    1882   Ueber die musik der Nordamericanischen
                      wilder. Leipzig, Breitkopf and Hartel.

Barrow, David C.
    1882   A Georgia corn-shucking. Century
                      Magazine 24:873-78.

Barton, William E.
    1898   Old plantation hymns. New England
                      Magazine 19:443-56.
    1899   Recent Negro melodies. New England
                      Magazine 19:707-19.

Birnie, C. W.
    1927   The education of the Negro in Charleston,
                      South Carolina before the war. Journal
                      of Negro History 12:5-13.

Blacknall, O. W.
    1883   The new departure in Negro life. Atlantic
                      Monthly 52:680-85.

Brackett, Jeffery E.
1890   The colored people of Maryland since
                    the war. In: Johns Hopkins University
                    Studies in Historical and Political
                    Science VII, Baltimore, Maryland.

Bradford, Alex
1957   Statement during performance.
                    Chicago, Illinois.

Bradley, Arthur G.
1879   A peep at the southern Negro.
                    Macmillans Magazine 39:61-68.

Brown, John
1859   Slave life in Georgia; a narrative of
                    the life, sufferings and escape of
                    John Brown a fugitive slave now in
                    England. Ed. by L. A. Chamerovzow.
                    London, the editor.

Brown, John M.
1868   Songs of the slave. Lippincotts
                    Magazine 2:617-23.

Brown, O.
1862   Letter dated Craney Island, Va.
                    December 31, 1862. Cited in
                    Emancipation League.

Brown, William W.
1880   My southern home. Boston, A. G. Brown
                    and Company.

Bruce, Phillip A.
1899   The plantation Negro as a freeman.
                    New York, G. P. Putnam's Sons.

Bryant, Winifred
1892   Negro services. The American Missionary
                    46:301-02.

Burlin, Natalie Curtis
1918-9   Hampton series of Negro folk-songs.
                    New York, G. Schirmer.

1919   Black singers and players. Musical
                    quarterly 5:86-89.

Cable, George W.
1885   The dance in Place Congo. Century
                    Magazine 21:807-27.

Cade, John B.
1935   Out of the mouth of slaves. Journal
                        of Negro History 20:294-337.

Chicago Commission on Race Relations
1922   The Negro in Chicago. Chicago,
                        University of Chicago Press.

Clarke, Milton and Lewis Clark
1846   Narrative of the sufferings of Lewis and
                        Milton Clarke, Boston, B. Marsh.

Cohen, Wilbur J.
1958   Current issues in social welfare.
                        Public Aid in Illinois 25:1-4.

Courlander, Harold
1939   Haiti singing. Chapel Hill, University
                        of North Carolina Press.

Daniels, John
1914   In freedom's birthplace. Boston, Houghton
                        Mifflin Company.

Davis, Allison, Burleigh Gardner and Mary R. Gardner
1941   Deep south. Chicago, University of Chicago
                        Press.

Dett, R. Nathaniel
1928   Religious folk-songs of the Negro.
                        American Journal of Sociology 33:989-95.

Dodge, David
1886   The free Negros of North Carolina.
                        Atlantic Monthly 57:23-30.

Dollard, John
1937   Caste and class in a southern town.
                        New Haven, Yale University Press.

Dorsey, Thomas A.
1956   Personal interview, Chicago, Illinois.
1957a   Personal interview, Chicago, Illinois.
1957b   Address to Annual Convention.

Drake, St. Claire
1940   Churches and voluntary associations in
                        Chicago Negro communities. Chicago,
                        Work Projects Administration, Illinois.

Drake, St. Clair and Horace R. Cayton
    1945   Black metropolis. New York, Harcourt,
                   Brace and Company.

Dubois, W. E. B.
    1902   The Negro in the black belt. Washington,
                   D. C. Department of Labor.
    1903   The Negro church. Atlanta, University
                   of Atlanta Press.

Edens, Boyce
    1917   When labor is cheap. Survey
                   (September 8, 1917, p.511).

Emancipation League
    1863   Facts concerning the freedmen. Boston,
                   Emancipation League.

Fenner, Thomas P.
    1874   Cabin and plantation songs as sung by
                   the Hampton students. In Armstrong and
                   Ludlow, Hampton and its students.

Fisher, Miles Mark
    1953   Negro Slave Songs in the United States.
                   Ithaca, Cornell University Press.
    1938   The Negro churches. Crisis 45:220, 239,
                   245.

Fisk University
    1945   Unwritten history of slavery. Nashville,
                   Fisk University Press.

Fitch, Charles
    1863   Letter dated January 1, 1863. In
                   Emancipation League 1863:9.

Flemming, Walter L.
    1905   The civil war and reconstruction in
                   Alabama. New York, Columbia University
                   Press.

Fontennette, Gus
    1955   Personal interview April 25, 1955.
                   Washington, D.C.

Foote, William H.
    1850   Sketches of Virginia. Philadelphia,
                   W. S. Martien.

Forten, C. L.
1864   Life on the Sea Islands. Atlantic Monthly
                13:587-94.

Franklin, John Hope
1947   From slavery to freedom. New York,
                A. A. Knopf.

Frederick, Francis
1869   Autobiography of Rev. Francis Frederick
                of Virginia, Baltimore, J. W. Woods.

Fukuyama, Yoshio
1955   South side study. (Mimeographed report)
                February 14, 1955. Department of Church
                Development and Commity of the Church
                Federation of Chicago.

Fuller, Thomas Oscar
1938   The story of church life among Negroes in
                Memphis, Tennessee. Memphis, Pictorial
                History, Inc.

Georgia Writers Project
1941   Drums and shadows, survival studies among
                Georgia coastal Negroes. Athens,
                University of Georgia.

Ginzberg, Eli
1956   The Negro potential. New York, Columbia
                University Press.

Gosnell, Harold F.
1935   Negro politicians. Chicago, University
                of Chicago Press.

Graham, Alice
1922   Original plantation melodies as one rarely
                hears them. Etude 40:744.

Greene, Lorenzo J.
1942   The Negro in colonial New England. New
                York, Columbia University Press.

Griffin, George H.
1882   The slave music of the south. American
                Missionary Magazine 36:70-72.

Haskell, Marion
1899   Negro spirituals. Century Magazine 58:
                577-81.

Herskovits, Frances S.
    1935   Dahomean Songs for the Dead. New
                    Republic 84:95.

Herskovits, Melville J.
    1937a   African gods and Catholic saints in New
                    World Negro belief. American Anthro-
                    pologist 38:635-43.
    1937b   Life in a Haitian Valley. New York,
                    A. A. Knopf.
    1944   Drums and drummers in Afro-Brazilian
                    cult life. Music Quarterly 30:477-92.
    1948   Man and his works. New York, A. A. Knopf.
    1952   Music in West Africa. (Pamphlet)
    1958   The myth of the Negro past. Reprint.
                    Boston, Beacon Press.

Herskovits, M. J. and Richard A. Waterman
    1949   Musica de culto Afro-bahiana.
                    Revista de Estudios Musicales 1:65-127.

Higginson, Thomas W.
    1870   Army life in a black regiment. Boston,
                    Fields, Osgood and Co.

Hooper, E. W.
    1863   Letter dated January 1, 1863. In Emanci-
                    pation League 1863:4.

Hornbostel, Erich von
    1905   Die Probleme der vergleichenden musik-
                    wissenschaft, Zeitschrift der Internationalen
                    Musikgesellschaft 7:85-97.
    1911   Uber ein akustichescriterium fur
                    kulturzusammenhange. Zeitschrift fur
                    ethnologie 43:601-15.
    1926   American Negro Songs. International Review
                    of Missions 15:748-53.
    1928   African Negro music. Africa 1:30-62.
    1936   Fuegian songs. American Anthropologist
                    38:357.

Howard, John T. Jr.
    1919   The spirit of the real Negro music.
                    The Musician 24:13.

Jackson, George Pullen
    1943   White and Negro spirituals. New York,
                    J. J. Augustin.

Jackson, Luther P.
        1931   Religious development of the Negro in
                        Virginia from 1760 to 1860. Journal
                        of Negro History 16:168-239.

Jackson, Mahalia
        1958   Personal interview, January 5, 1958.
                        Chicago, Illinois.

Johnson, Guion G.
        1930   A social history of the Sea Islands.
                        Chapel Hill, the University of North
                        Carolina Press.

Johnson, Guy B.
        1931   The Negro spiritual; a problem in
                        Anthropology. American Anthropologist
                        33:151-57.
        1936   Recent contributions to the study of
                        American Negro songs. Social Forces
                        4:788-92.

Johnson, James W.
        1926   The second book of Negro spirituals.
                        New York, Viking Press.
        1929   Negro folksongs and spirituals.
                        Mentor 17:50-52.
        1944   The history of the Negro spirituals.
                        In Sylvestre C. Watkins, An Anthology
                        of American Negro Literature, New York,
                        Random House, Inc.

Jordan, L. G.
        1905   What the brethern in black are doing.
                        The Missionary Review of the World,
                        28:599-602.

Kemble, Frances A.
        1863   Journal of a residence of a Georgia
                        plantation in 1838-1839. New York,
                        Harper and Brothers.

Kennedy, Louise V.
        1930   The Negro peasant turns cityward. New
                        York, Columbia University Press.

Kennedy, R. Emmet
        1924   Black cameos. New York, Albert and
                        Charles Boni.

Ketcham, George F.
1951   The Yearbook of American Churches. New
              York, National Council of the Churches
              of Christ in the U.S.A.

Kilham, Elizabeth
1870   Sketches in color.   Putnam's Magazine
              15:31-38, 304-11.

King, Edward
1875   The great South. Hartford, Connecticut,
              American Publishing Co.

Kirby, P. R.
1930   A study of Negro Harmony.   Musical
              Quarterly 16:404-14.

Kolinski, Mieczyslaw
1936   Suriname Music. In Melville J. and
              Frances S. Herskovits, Suriname Folklore.
              New York, Columbia University Press.
1949   La musica del Oeste Africano. Revista
              de Estudios Musicales 1:208,210.

Krehbiel, Henry Edward
1914   Afro-american folksongs. London, New
              York, Schirmer.

Landis, Benson Y.
1958   Yearbook of American churches. National
              Council of the Churches of Christ in
              the U.S.A.

Laubenstein, P. F.
1930   Race values in Afroamerican music. Music
              Quarterly 16:378-403.

Longini, Muriel D.
1939   Folksongs of Chicago Negroes. Journal
              of American Folklore 53:96-111.

MacLean, Amie B.
1903   Three churches in Deland, Florida. In
              Duboise (Ed.) The Negro church. Atlanta,
              Atlanta University Press.

Macrae, David
1870   The Americans at home, Vol. I. Edinburgh,
              Edmonston and Douglas.

Malet, William W.
    1863   An errand to the south in the summer
                        of 1862. London, R. Bentley.

Marsh, J. B. T.
    1892   The story of the jubilee singers.
                        Boston, Houghton.

Mays, Benjamin E. and Joseph W. Nicholos
    1933   The Negro's church. New York, Institute
                        of Social and Religious Research.

McAllester, David P.
    1949   Peyote music. New York, Viking Fund
                        Publications in Anthropology.

McCutchan, Robert G.
    1945   Hymns in the live of men. New York,
                        Abingdon-Cokesbury Press.

McIllheny, E. A.
    1910   Befo' de war spirituals. Boston, The
                        Christopher Publishing House.

McKay, Claude
    1940   Harlem; Negro metropolis. New York,
                        E. P. Dutton and Company.

Merriam, Alan P.
    1951   Songs of the Afro-Bahian cults; an
                        ethnomusicological analysis. Ph. D.
                        Dissertation, Northwestern University,
                        Department of Anthropology.
    1952   The African background. The Record
                        Changer (Nov. 1952:7-8).
    1955a   The use of music in the study of a
                        problem of acculturation. American
                        Anthropologist 57:28-34.
    1955b   Music in American culture. American
                        Anthropologist 57:1173-81.
    1957a   Africa south of the Sahara (Pamphlet).
    1957b   Yovu songs from Ruanda. Zaire (November-
                        December 1957:933-66).

Merriam, Alan P. and Linton C. Freeman
    1956   Statistical classification in anthropology;
                        an application to ethnomusicology. American
                        Anthropologist 53:464-72.

Merriam, Alan P., Sarah Whinery and Behnard Fred
    1956   Songs of a Rada Community in Trinidad.
                Anthropos 51:57-174.

Morris, Kenneth
    1956   Personal interview, Chicago, Illinois.

Murphy, Jeannette R.
    1899   The survival of African music in America.
                Appleton's Popular Science Monthly
                55:660-72.

Myrdal, Gunnar
    1944   An American dilemma. New York, Harper
                and Brothers.

Niles, John J.
    1927   Singing soldiers. New York, C. Scribner's
                Sons.

Nordhoff, Charles
    1876   The cotton states in the spring and summer
                of 1875. New York, D. Appleton and Com-
                pany.

Odum, Howard
    1876   Swing low sweet chariot. Country
                Gentleman 91:18-19.

Odum, Howard and Guy B. Johnson
    1925   The Negro and his songs. Chapel Hill,
                University of North Carolina Press.

Olmstead, Frederick L.
    1856   A journey in the seaboard slave states
                1853-54, II. New York, Dix and Edwards.

Ortiz, Fernando
    1952   Los instrumentos de la musica Afrocubana.
                Havana, Publicaciones de la direccion de
                Cultura del Ministerio de Educacion. Five
                volumes.

Parrish, Lydia A.
    1942   Slave songs of the Georgia Sea Islands.
                New York, Creative Age Press.

Peabody, Charles
    1904   Notes on Negro music. Southern Workman
                33:305-09.

411.

Phillips, U. B.
1910   A documentary history of American industrial society. Cleveland, A. H. Clark
Company.

Pipes, William H.
1951   Say Amen Brother. New York, William-
Frederick Press.

Proctor, Henry H.
1907   The theology of the songs of the southern
slave. Southern Workman 36:584-92.

Powdermaker, Hortense
1939   After freedom. New York, The Viking
Press.

Raper, Arthur
1936   A preface to peasantry. Chapel Hill,
University of North Carolina Press.

Reed, Ira De A.
1926   Let us pray. Opportunity (September
1926, pp. 274-75).

Reed, Richard Clark
1914   A sketch of the religious history of the
Negroes in the South. In Rockwell (Ed.),
Papers of the American Society of Church
History IV, New York.

Robinson, F. L.
1889a   The coloured people of the United States
(South). Leisure Hour 38:54-59.
1889b   The coloured people of the United States
(North). Leisure Hour 38:697-99.

Robinson, Rev. Nina
1951   Statement. In Minutes of the Nineteenth
Annual Session National Convention Gospel
Choirs and Choruses, Inc.

Rogers, James
1867   Notes cited in Allen, Ware and Garrison,
p. 47.

Russell, John H.
1913   The free Negro in Virginia in 1619-1895.
Baltimore, Johns Hopkins University Press.

Ryder, C. J.
1892   The theology of the plantation songs.
            The American Missionary 46:9-16.

Sayer, Samuel
1863   Letter dated January 2, 1863. In
            Emancipation League.

Scarborough, Dorothy
1925   On the trail of Negro folk-songs.
            Cambridge, Harvard University Press.

Seward, Theodore
1872   Jubilee Songs. New York, Bigelow.

Showers, Susan
1898   A weddin' and a burial. New England
            Magazine 18:478-83.

Simms, James M.
1888   The first colored church in America.
            Philadelphia, J. B. Lippincott.

Snyder, Howard
1920   A plantation revival service. Yale
            Review 10:169-72.

Spaulding, H. G.
1863   Under the palmetto. Continental Monthly
            2:188-203.

Stearnes, Charles
1872   The black man of the South and the
            rebels. Boston, N. E. News Company.

Stetson, G. R.
1877   The southern Negro as he is. Boston,
            G. H. Ellis.

Stewart, Austin
1857   Twenty-two years a slave and forty years
            a freeman. Rochester W. Alling.

Stillman, C. A.
1879   The freedman in the United States. Catho-
            lic Presbyterian 1:119-27.

Stone, Alfred H.
1908   Studies in the American race problem.
            New York, Doubleday, Page and Company.

Turner, Edward R.
    1911   The Negro in Pennsylvania 1639-1861.
                  Washington, D. C., The American
                  Historical Association.

United States Bureau of the Census
    1860   Eighth census, population, I.
    1870   Ninth census, population, I.
    1910   Thirteenth census, population, I,II.
    1915   Bulletin 120, The Negro in the United
                  States 1790-1915.
    1920   Fourteenth census, population, II.
    1930   Fifteenth census, population, II.
    1935   Census of Religious Bodies.
    1940   Sixteenth census, population, II.
                  part I.
    1943   Special report P1943, No. 4.
    1950   Special report P-E 3B.

Wallaschek, Richard
    1893   Primitive music. New York, Longmans,
                  Green and Company.

Waterman, Richard A.
    1943   African patterns in Trinidad Negro music.
                  Ph. D. Diss. Northwestern University,
                  Department of Anthropology.
    1948   'Hot' rhythm in Negro music. Journal of
                  the American Musicological Society 1:3-16.
    1951   Gospel hymns of a Negro church in Chicago.
                  Journal of the International Folk Music
                  Council 3:87-93.
    1952   African influence on the music of the
                  Americas. In Sol Tax (Ed.), Acculturation
                  in the Americas, Chicago, University of
                  Chicago Press.

Watson, John F.
    1846   Annals of occurrences of New York City
                  and State. Philadelphia, H. F. Anners.

Warner, Robert A.
    1940   New Haven Negroes. New Haven, Yale
                  University Press.

White, Newman I.
    1928   American Negro folk-songs. Cambridge,
                  Harvard University Press.

Wilder, C. B.
    1863   Letter dated December 30, 1862. In
                  Emancipation League 1863.

Windom, A. B.
    1951   Statement in Minutes of the Nineteenth
                Annual Session National Convention Gospel
                Choirs and Choruses, Inc.

Woodson, Carter G.
    1921   The history of the Negro church.
                Washington, D.C., The Associated Publishers.
    1930   The rural Negro. Washington, D.C., The
                Associated Publishers.

Woofter, Thomas J.
    1928   Negro problems in cities. New York,
                Doubleday, Doran.

Work, John W.
    1949   Changing patterns of Negro folk songs.
                Journal of American Folklore 62:135-44.

APPENDIX

415.

MODAL STRUCTURES OF SPIRITUALS

MODAL STRUCTURES OF JUBILEES

MODAL STRUCTURES OF GOSPELS

VITA

GEORGE ROBINSON RICKS

Born: WASHINGTON, D. C., OCTOBER 9, 1924

HOWARD UNIVERSITY, WASHINGTON, D. C., 1941-1942

TUSKEGEE INSTITUTE, TUSKEGEE, ALABAMA, 1943
(College Training Detachment, Army Air Force)

NORTHWESTERN UNIVERSITY, EVANSTON, ILLINOIS, 1945-1948 B.Mus.Ed.

NORTHWESTERN UNIVERSITY, EVANSTON, ILLINOIS, 1949   M. Mus.

INTERNATIONAL FOLKLORE

An Arno Press Collection

Allies, Jabez. **On The Ancient British, Roman, and Saxon Antiquities and Folk-Lore of Worcestershire.** 1852

Blair, Walter and Franklin J. Meine, editors. **Half Horse Half Alligator.** 1956

Bompas, Cecil Henry, translator. **Folklore of the Santal Parganas.** 1909

Bourne, Henry. **Antiquitates Vulgares; Or, The Antiquities of the Common People.** 1725

Briggs, Katharine Mary. **The Anatomy of Puck.** 1959

Briggs, Katharine Mary. **Pale Hecate's Team.** 1962

Brown, Robert. **Semitic Influence in Hellenic Mythology.** 1898

Busk, Rachel Harriette. **The Folk-Songs of Italy.** 1887

Carey, George. **A Faraway Time and Place.** 1971

Christiansen, Reidar Th. **The Migratory Legends.** 1958

Clouston, William Alexander. **Flowers From a Persian Garden, and Other Papers.** 1890

Colcord, Joanna Carver. **Sea Language Comes Ashore.** 1945

Dorson, Richard Mercer, editor. **Davy Crockett.** 1939

Douglas, George Brisbane, editor. **Scottish Fairy and Folk Tales.** 1901

Gaidoz, Henri and Paul Sébillot. **Blason Populaire De La France.** 1884

Gardner, Emelyn Elizabeth. **Folklore From the Schoharie Hills, New York.** 1937

Gill, William Wyatt. **Myths and Songs From The South Pacific.** 1876

Gomme, George Laurence. **Folk-Lore Relics of Early Village Life.** 1883

Grimm, Jacob and Wilhelm. **Deutsche Sagen.** 1891

Gromme, Francis Hindes. **Gypsy Folk-Tales.** 1899

Hambruch, Paul. **Faraulip.** 1924

Ives, Edward Dawson. **Larry Gorman.** 1964

Jansen, William Hugh. **Abraham "Oregon" Smith.** 1977

Jenkins, John Geraint. **Studies in Folk Life.** 1969

Kingscote, Georgiana and Pandit Natêsâ Sástrî, compilers. **Tales of the Sun.** 1890

Knowles, James Hinton. **Folk-Tales of Kashmir.** 1893

Lee, Hector Haight. **The Three Nephites.** 1949

MacDougall, James, compiler. **Folk Tales and Fairy Lore in Gaelic and English.** 1910

Mather, Increase. **Remarkable Providences Illustrative of the Earlier Days of American Colonisation.** 1856

McNair, John F.A. and Thomas Lambert Barlow. **Oral Tradition From the Indus.** 1908

McPherson, Joseph McKenzie. **Primitive Beliefs in the North-East of Scotland.** 1929

Miller, Hugh. **Scenes and Legends of the North of Scotland.** 1869

Müller, Friedrich Max. **Comparative Mythology.** 1909

Palmer, Abram Smythe. **The Samson-Saga and Its Place in Comparative Religion.** 1913

Parker, Henry. **Village Folk-Tales of Ceylon.** Three volumes. 1910-1914

Parkinson, Thomas. **Yorkshire Legends and Traditions.** 1888

Perrault, Charles. **Popular Tales.** 1888

Rael, Juan B. **Cuentos Españoles de Colorado y Nuevo Méjico.** Two volumes. 1957

Ralston, William Ralston Shedden. **Russian Folk-Tales.** 1873

Rhys Davids, Thomas William, translator. **Buddhist Birth Stories; Or, Jātaka Tales.** 1880

Ricks, George Robinson. **Some Aspects of the Religious Music of the United States Negro.** 1977

Swynnerton, Charles. **Indian Nights' Entertainment, Or Folk-Tales From the Upper Indus.** 1892

Sydow, Carl Wilhelm von. **Selected Papers on Folklore.** 1948

Taliaferro, Harden E. **Fisher's River (North Carolina) Scenes and Characters.** 1859

Temple, Richard Carnac. **The Legends of the Panjâb.** Three volumes. 1884-1903

Tully, Marjorie F. and Juan B. Rael. **An Annotated Bibliography of Spanish Folklore in New Mexico and Southern Colorado.** 1950

Wratislaw, Albert Henry, translator. **Sixty Folk-Tales From Exclusively Slavonic Sources.** 1889

Yates, Norris W. **William T. Porter and the Spirit of the Times.** 1957